# JOURNEY TOWARD WHOLENESS

MW01283447

## A HISTORY OF BLACK DISCIPLES OF CHRIST IN THE MISSION OF THE CHRISTIAN CHURCH

**VOL. 1**
From Convention
to Convocation:
No Longer
'Objects of' Mission
But
'Partners In'
the Work
(1700-1988)

by
**BRENDA M. CARDWELL**
and
**WILLIAM K. FOX, SR.**

This series is sponsored and published by the Board of Trustees of the
National Convocation of the Christian Church (Disciples of Christ), 1990

Revised by GWD Ministries with indexing constructed by
Dr. David Ian McWhirter 2005

Printed in the USA.

# TABLE OF CONTENTS

## From Convention to Convocation:
## No Longer 'Objects of' Mission
## But 'Partners In' the Work (1700-1988)

# PROLOGUE

## by William K. Fox, Sr.

"Inasmuch as many have undertaken to compile a narrative of
the things which have been accomplished among us by those
who from the beginning were eye witnesses and ministers
of the word, it seemed good to me also, having followed all
things closely for some time past, to write an orderly account
for you... that you may know the truth concerning the things
which you have been informed"
—*Luke 1:1-4. (RSV)*

From the mid-1940's through the 1960's, leadership of the Christian
Church (Disciples of Christ) endeavored to lead the body politic from
a racial separatist position toward racial integration—meaning mainly
African-Anglo integration. Within the late 1960's and early 1970's a
more ultimate goal was added called "wholeness in the Church."

The concept of "wholeness" supersedes that of racial integration. It
gives recognition of the pluralistic nature of human society. Biblical
foundation is found in the image of the Christian community cited in
the Acts of the Apostles and the Letters of Paul.

Thus today the Christian Church (Disciples of Christ) has come to view
African and Anglo-Americans as two of several racial and/or ethnic
groups which constitute the totality of the Christian community—the
whole Church.

However, whether one advocates the racial integration stance, the
ultimate goal of wholeness, or a combination of the two, one must
understand that two distinctive racial and/or ethnic dimensions do
exist. Each dimension has a history and development, which should
be understood, appreciated, and allowed to intermingle with the other.
The result will be a whole Church, which manifests the Holy Spirit and
the servanthood of Jesus the Christ.

In 1986 the Board of Trustees of the National Convocation of the
Christian Church (Disciples of Christ) responded to a challenge from
Administrative Secretary John Foulkes and President Alvin O. Jackson,

to sponsor a massive historical research project dealing with the life and service of African-American Disciples of Christ. The proposal called for the engagement of several persons to systematically assemble and develop a series of volumes on the subject.

I was asked to be the editor and initiate the series. The intention is to take into account every good work already completed, as well as the utilization of other research documents, knowledge and experiences which were available. The series is being published under the broad leading of JOURNEY TOWARD WHOLENESS. It should present a comprehensive picture.

From Convention to Convocation: No Longer 'Objects of' Mission But 'Partners In' the Work (1700-1988), is the first volume of the series. It is a general history of the National Christian Missionary Convention/ National Convocation of the Christian Church (Disciples of Christ).

Brenda Cardwell's Master of Divinity thesis in 1981 at Lexington Theological Seminary, Lexington, Kentucky entitled, Three Concerns of Black Disciples From 1917 TO 1969, has provided a basis for several aspects of this historical treatment.[1] Cardwell's thesis deals with (1) the Concern for Education, (2) Concern with Struggle and Alienation and (3) Concern for the Restructure of the National Christian Missionary Convention.

References from the thesis have been used which relate to some of the actions and work of the National Christian Missionary Convention/ National Convocation of the Christian Church (Disciples of Christ). I have collaborated with her in the rewriting of some of these aspects and in the expansion of the original thesis design.

Beside the utilization of formalized sources of documentation, information has come from interviews of contemporary actors in the church, unpublished papers, correspondence files and related materials.

Special reference is made to James Blair's 1958 Bachelor of Divinity thesis entitled, The National Convention Facing Integration.[2] This document became a principal reference when we dealt with the early years of the National Christian Missionary Convention. It was one of the first attempts by an African-American Disciples of Christ scholar to write a serious history of the National Christian Missionary Convention.

In addition, I have drawn upon my own files and extensive experience as one of the principal actors in the life and work of the Convention/Convocation from 1960 through 1982.

At this point in history we celebrate the fact that several among us-both African-American and Anglo-American- are taking the study and recording of the faith journey of Black Disciples of Christ seriously.

## CHAPTER ONE

# BACKGROUND FOR DISCIPLES OF CHRIST MISSION AMONG AFRICAN-AMERICANS

Thanksgiving season is a time when our past acts of the year stab our conscience. Like a stinging arrow it gives sudden insight into some tangled area of our living. The American white man has found it is much easier to be prosperous than it is to be civilized...

It would be better if all whites could suddenly turn black and blacks white. Then one group would find out what it means to be in the others place...

Two hundred and forty-five years of labor of the black man without a pay day is not too long for him to give thanks that he is in a country such as we had in 1865. It was the prayers of our forefathers and the few white Christians which gave us our freedom...
—*Merle R. Eppse, Black Disciples of Christ historian and editor of "The Christian Plea", editorial, Fall, 1940.*

The National Christian Missionary Convention did not soar out of the plains of church history full blown. Its roots lie deep in the socio-religious milieu of the critically oppressive and dark eighteenth century United States slave culture as well as of the beginnings of the industrial society in the late nineteenth and early twentieth century.

Its sprouts spring from the swirling currents of social change which rippled from the historic struggle of the War Between the States. Hard against this backdrop were biblical references like the following which were among the watchwords of every devout Disciple of Christ: "For as many of you as were baptized into Christ have put on Christ. There is neither Jew nor Greek, there is neither slave nor free, there is neither male nor female; for you all are one in Christ Jesus" (Galatians 3:27-28).

But African-American Disciples of Christ—like all other Black members in the Christian faith- whether Protestant or Roman Catholic—were born out of struggle and alienation. Their forefathers and mothers were brought against their will to the shores of the New World in North America. They were stripped of their native clothes, language, customs, folkways and religion. And as mortals considered less than human, they were considered material possessions to be battered and bartered, used and enslaved, sold for profit to the highest bidder.

Little wonder that when the Church of that day looked over the world for a fertile mission field, they saw the enslaved Black person in the United States not so much as a child of God to be, but too often as an object of mission to be secured like cattle in order to raise the material value of the Christian estate. A complete understanding of the rationale for the organization of the Christian Missionary Convention and the function of the National Convocation of the Christian Church (Disciples of Christ) requires an appreciation of this slave culture and the prevailing concept of mission effort among African-Americans at the dawn of the twentieth century.

## BORN OUT OF ALIENATION AND STRUGGLE

James Blair is most correct when he reminds us that there was a direct relationship between slavery and the Restoration Movement.[1] Benchmarks in the history of the Disciples of Christ in the United States scene are (1) the Cane Ridge Revival of 1801; (2) the Last Will and Testament of the Springfield Presbytery at Cane Ridge, which was signed by leaders in June 1804, and (3) the organization of the Christian Association of Washington in August 1809. Each of these signal events in the formation of the Christian Church (Disciples of Christ) occurred during the period of United States slavery.

Records of this dark epoch in United States history show that many of the leaders like Alexander Campbell and Barton W. Stone, who led during the early years of the Christian Church (Disciples of Christ), were slaveholders.

By 1850 the Disciples had 310 churches in the South and 543 congregations in the North. The annual report of the American and

Foreign Anti-slavery Society says... that the "Campbellites owned 101,000 slaves, the Methodists twice that number, and the Baptists only a few more. If this is true, the Disciples, on a per capita basis, constituted the leading slaveholders in the nation.[2]

But there had been an accretion of cultural values among African-Americans long before Anglo-American Christians sought to evangelize them. They had gained a high regard for family and blood kinship, a religious mind-set which was wed to a belief in the things of spirit within the affairs of life in the real world; a sense of working together with the spiritual forces in the world, a confidence in the wisdom of the group's council of elders, and a belief in the medicine man's solution and treatment of the ills of the body.

However, more than a century before the Disciples of Christ made attempts to evangelize African-Americans, United States Protestant and Roman Catholic missionaries had witnessed among Blacks. Blacks had become established leaders of there own congregations and church structures. The religious background of some of the Black Disciples of Christ leaders who organized conventions in the states and later guided the launching of the National Christian Missionary Convention included prior membership in some of these denominational groups, notably Baptists and Methodists. Many others were brought into the Christian Church through the influence of their slaveowners who were members of the Restoration movement.

Andrew Jackson Hurdle, the noted father of Disciples of Christ ministers in Texas, was born into slavery on Christmas Day, 1847. When he was ten years old he was separated from his parents and brought to Texas as the slave of T. H. Turner of Dangerfield who apparently belonged to the Restoration movement. From an unpublished history of the Black Texas Christian Missionary Convention by his son, I. Q. Hurdle, it is not clear as to what church affiliation he had while a slave. But it seems that he became a Disciple through a brush harbor evangelistic meeting.

Sarah Lue Bostick of Little Rock, Arkansas, the noted African-American Disciples pioneer in home missions, joined the Baptist church in 1884 in Monroe County, Kentucky. When her first husband died in 1888 she went to live with some of her family in Arkansas. It was at Pea Ridge Christian Church in Arkansas that she became a member of the Disciples of Christ.

William Alphin, a major force in the establishment of the National Christian Missionary Convention, and later one of its field staff, grew up with his parents as a devout Baptist. But as a youth he became dissatisfied with the idea that Christians had to be called "Baptists" when he discovered they "were called Christians first at Antioch" (Acts 11:26). So he, and later his entire family, joined Beech Grove Christian Church in Tennessee.

Sere Stacy "S.S." Myers, is a noted African-American Disciples of Christ church strategist and architect of the merger of program and staff services for the National Christian Missionary Convention and the United Christian Missionary Society. He was born September 25, 1898 in Clay County, Mississippi to ex-slave parents who were devout Baptists. Myer's father, Frank, was a faithful deacon at Hopewell Baptist Church for 52 years and earnestly wanted his son to be a Baptist minister.

S.S. Myers received his high school education at Southern Christian Institute in Edwards, Mississippi and graduated as valedictorian of his class. He joined the Christian Church (Disciples of Christ) and later was ordained into its ministry.

Robert Hayes Peoples, pioneer African-American pastor, national staff and Convention leader, was born January 25, 1903 in Hollywood, Mississippi, and grew up in the Baptist church. Like Myers, Peoples was introduced to the Restoration movement while a student at Southern Christian Institute. Following ordination he was one of the few Blacks in Christian ministry to prepare for larger Christian service at Eureka College in Eureka, Illinois.

But African-Americans had been heavily influenced by other Protestant bodies many years before the Restoration movement was born! The missionary activities of the various religious groups among slaves during the middle part of the seventeenth century up to the first half of the eighteenth set the background for how the churches responded to slavery and the Civil War, they also showed how African-Americans were to fare within the church following the end of that war. The Church of England under William III, the Moravians, Methodists, Baptists, Presbyterians, Friends, and Roman Catholics made special thrusts toward the enslaved African-American people.

The Society for the Propagation of the Gospel in Foreign Parts was organized by the Church of England on June 16, 1701. This society sent Samuel Thomas and Dr. Le Jean to South Carolina where they instructed Black people from 1702 to 1714.[3]

Although Methodists did not come to this country in any substantial number until 1766, Mr. Fillmore, one of their missionaries, reported the impressive assembly of a "number of Blacks" in his meetings. The Great Revival carried on in Virginia and North Carolina between 1773 and 1776 by the Methodists and the Episcopal Church won hundreds of Blacks to Christianity.[4]

In 1779 Methodists joined with the Presbyterians and Baptists in spreading the spiritual fervor of the Great Awakening of Kentucky to slaves throughout the South. Three to four thousand African-Americans were won to Christianity. The Methodists were zealous in their activity. In 1786 they started the idea of a separate roll of African-American communicants. By 1815 they had a Black membership of 43,187.

Baptists were equally as determined in their approach. The first African-American Baptist church was organized in Petersburg, Virginia, in 1776.[5] by 1803, 18,000 Blacks were enrolled in their communions through direct associations. Many African-American preachers were appointed to serve their own people (and sometimes Whites) on plantations.

If the complete outline of history was given here, it would include similar efforts by Presbyterians, Congregationalists, Lutherans, Moravians, and Roman Catholics. Although religion has always been regarded as the Black slave's sole source of consolation, there is evidence that, in some instances, slaves had some distressing experiences in attempting to enjoy the soothing fruits of religious living. A certain White Baptist preacher in Mississippi was known to compel "his slaves to labor on the Sabbath, and justified himself under the plea that if they were not at work they would be sporting, roving about the fields and woods, thereby desecrating the Sabbath more than by laboring under an overseer.[6]

On one occasion in South Carolina, two planters were dining together while discussing the sincerity of the professions of religion by slaves. One said that such professons were authentic and the other said, he had a slave who would die rather than deny the Redeemer. He called this slave to him and tried to induce him to deny his Savior. When he refused he was whipped terribly. He died (for his Savior) as a consequence of this severe infliction.[7]

Another story is told of an old Black slave in Portsmouth, Virginia who came under deep conviction for sin. Therefore he went into the back part of his owner's garden to pour out his soul in prayer to God. "For this offence he was whipped with thirty-nine lashes."[8]

Out of the silent tears and suffering of these years there emerged the African-American preacher and church. This was possibly the greatest institutional development among Black people. It came into being long before the launching of the Christian Church (Disciples of Christ) and the founding of the National Christian Missionary Convention.

Under the guidance of slave preachers, the church became the means by which most slaves survived the plantation system and the subsequent ensnarlement in an agricultural economy supported largely by sharecropping, renting and day laborers. Slave preachers were believed to be divine prophets who had received the "call." They held a powerful sway over the people. Therefore they were considered by Whites to be a valuable means of keeping slaves contented. As long as they told the people about a God in the heavens who would come, by and by, and relieve them of their troubles if they kept on praying, White slaveholders knew they had nothing to fear from the rising slave population.

However, the upsurge of the slave minister's influence over African-Americans came to a disastrous climax in the insurrection movement which was launched in 1800 by Gabriel Prosser. It continued with Denmark Vessey in 1822 and ended with the ill-conceived adventure of Nat Turner at South Hampton, Virginia, in 1831. But these cataclysmic excursions of slaves being led in revolt under the direction of African-American preachers only underscored the importance of these ministers.

When industrialization and World War I took place, there was the steady migration of African-Americans from the rural South to the industrializing North and eventually to the West. Throughout the period of the great migration, the African-American minister and church became the integrative center of experience. The Christian community and church was a "refuge and strength." It was the river of God into which they could dip their tired bodies and rise with renewed strength to survive in a hostile environment.

The church was a place for celebration, praise, fellowship and thanksgiving to God. The worship services then—and in the traditional African-American churches now— was the basic expression of "church."

So when the Christian Church (Disciples of Christ) made its pitch toward African-American people in the mid-nineteenth century, they were addressing many thousands who were already in the church and thousands more who at least had heard about the Christian way. Many possessed a religious experience, and the principal leader, beside the local teacher was the African-American preacher.

## EARLY AFRICAN-AMERICAN DISCIPLES INITIATIVES

African-Americans were evangelizing one another and organizing Disciples of Christ congregations long before White Disciples made an organized approach to win them to the Movement. Strong Black Disciples of Christ congregations existed in most of the cotton states and parts of the Midwest at least 35 years before the organization of the National Christian Missionary Convention in 1917.

Many African-Americans, however, were brought into the Christian Church (Disciples of Christ) through the sincere efforts of Anglo-American Disciples church leaders. Isaiah Quit Hurdle's unpublished account of his father's start in the Christian Church is one illustration of how this was sometimes done.

Randolph Clark in August 1865 founded a colony of Freed men near Mt. Vernon. Each had a spot of land given by a slaveholder at the time of emancipation, June 19, 1865, and were building brush houses. Randolph Clark visited, made friends and distributed illustrated literature, taught them to sing hymns. He told them, "You are now free from slavery but you are not free from sin."

First converts were Mrs. Mary Johnson and her son-in-law, Andrew Jackson Hurdle. Elder Clark urged Christians to continue worshipping together. A. J. Hurdle was selected as parson. In Spring, 1866, Randolph and Addison Clark visited, ordained A. J. Hurdle as pastor. The Clarks continued to visit.[9]

The Hurdles went on to organize Clark Street Church in Greenville and the Christian Church in Center Point, Texas.

Oftentimes African-American congregations, which came into being via the cooperation of nearby predominantly Anglo-American congregations, were named "Second Christian" churches. Usually the

African-American members formerly worshipped in the predominantly Anglo-American congregation. Caught up in the benevolent spirit of evangelism, the Anglo-American congregation, through one or more of its affluent members, would secure a piece of land and facility where African-Americans could form their own congregation.

Not all of the early established African-American Disciples congregations were called "Second" churches. Many sprung up in the homes of devout, highly motivated African-American Christians who were eager to have congregations that were New Testament based and propagating the same doctrine heralded in the Restoration movement.

Good examples of such congregations can be found in the Piedmont Tri-State District Convention area of Virginia, North Carolina and West Virginia. During the last decade of the nineteenth century, Black Disciples of Christ founded First Christian Church in Stuart, Virginia (1888-89); First Christian Church in Reidsville, North Carolina (1893); and First Christian Church in Concord, North Carolina (1897).[10]

Many other congregations were established throughout the South which took on Bible names and/or the names of a particular rural or town area like Mt. Sinai, Pine Grove, New Bethel, Pea Ridge, Mt. Carmel, Cherry Hill, etc.

Some of the African-American Disciples of Christ leaders who were well experienced in church leadership before the Church made an intentional effort to reach them, these persons had secured freedom before the end of the Civil War. Moses Graves was one. He fled Kentucky through the Underground Railroad on to Canada. There he worked until the end of the War. He returned to Kentucky to get his wife, Eliza and their fourteen children. Then, along with his brothers, Chinn and Jackson and their families, he traveled west by covered wagons. They settled in the western states of Nebraska, Missouri and Kansas.[11] Out of their seed sprang many lay leaders and ministers who served the church in those states and throughout the mid-South.

African-American area and state substructures, district and state conventions were organized by African-Americans in the mid-to-late nineteenth century at the very time a dedicated few Anglo-American leaders in the Christian Church were advocating cooperative mission work.

Early in their history, African-American Disciples of Christ within their own districts, states and areas became concerned about evangelism, better Sunday schools, and general education. In addition, there was a desperate need for fellowship, encouragement and a sense of community and support. It was mainly for these reasons that they formed fellowship meetings and conventions. Those organizations which have survived have usually fostered efforts to achieve specific church mission objectives that are most relevant to that area or state. Here is a listing of some of these organizations. Most were formed before the National Christian Missionary Convention and before any significant organized national support was given from the Christian Church (Disciples of Christ).

The following table reveals what was happening in the development of the Restoration movement among African-Americans in the United States. The facts document a trend of state and regional organization of predominantly African-American congregations. Often local and regional Anglo-American Disciples leaders cooperated in the organization. (see Table 1 on next page)

Prior to World War I there was minimal awareness of the large number of Black Disciples of Christ congregations dispersed among the several states who might be gathered together into a national body. Only on the Eastern Seaboard, where at the dawn of the twentieth century the migration of African-Americans to the north was most pronounced, did there seem to be an embryonic awareness of African-American Disciples of Christ as a growing movement.

Unfortunately, there was the development of a whole body of predominantly Black Disciples of Christ congregations that had little or no relationship to Afro-American Disciples of Christ growing up in the Cotton Belt states, the Midwest and the North. This dichotomy in development and orientation to the Restoration movement continued for many years.

It underscored another reason why the early leaders felt the necessity for organizing a truly National Christian Missionary Convention which would help all African-American Disciples of Christ feel a sense of community and Christian comradeship.

## TABLE 1

## ORGANIZED BLACK DISCIPLES OF CHRIST SUB-STRUCTURES

| ORGANIZATION | ORIGIN | ORIGINAL GOALS |
|---|---|---|
| Southern District of Churches of Christ, (D.O.C.) | 1867 | Evangelism: follow African- Americans into towns |
| National Convention of Disciples (Colored) Rufus Conrad, founder | 1867 | Evangelism and nurture |
| Kentucky Christian Missionary Convention | 1872 | Fellowship/nurture School/headquarters |
| Alabama Christian Missionary Convention | 1880 | Fellowship/nurture Cultural survival |
| Texas Christian Missionary Convention | 1881 | Black college/leadership: fellowship/nurture |
| Goldsboro-Raleigh Assembly Goldsboro, (West of Tarr River) | 1882 | Training school for lay and clergy |
| Piedmont Tri-State District Convention | 1882 | Training/school/ campground/staff |
| Mississippi Christian Missionary Convention | 1887 | Fellowship/nurture: Cultural survival |
| Western District of Churches of Christ, (D.O.C.) | 1892 | Evangelism |
| Washington and Norfolk District of Churches of Christ, (D.O.C.) (East of Tarr River) | 1910 | Evangelism: follow African-American Migration |
| First General Assembly of Goldsboro-Raleigh and Washington Colored Disciples of Christ in North Carolina | 1914 | Coordination of growing work among the churches |
| Quadrennial Assembly of the Church of Christ, (D.O.C.) | 1917 | Fellowship, inspiration, evangelism |
| Christian Women's Missionary Convention of the Churches of Christ, (D.O.C.) | 1926 | Home and foreign missions |
| The Northeastern District of Church of Christ, (D.O.C.) | 1929 | Evangelism: follow African-American migration |
| Biennial Assembly of the Churches of Christ, (D.O.C.) (Supplanting Quadrennial) | 1967 | Efficiency of operation |
| United Assembly of Church of Christ, (D.O.C.) | 1975 | Internal tensions within Northeastern District |

# CHAPTER TWO

# BACKGROUND ON THE CALL TO ORGANIZE THE NATIONAL CONVENTION

"For as many of you as were baptized into Christ have put on Christ. There is neither Jew nor Greek, there is neither slave nor free, there is neither male nor female; for all are one in Christ Jesus."
—*Galatians 3:27-28*

Although a great biblical truth, this truth has not always been a part of our actions. Even though the scriptures spoke, White Disciples of Christ in leadership positions were very silent. During the formative years of the American Christian Missionary Society there were calls for African-American Disciples of Christ to form their own national convention. Blacks desired greater cooperation, self-development and equality in the life of the Disciples of Christ movement. African-Anglo relationships were usually steeped in paternalism, inequality, distrust, or passivism.

After the freeing of Blacks from slavery in the mid 1800's, African-Americans became objects of mission. It was seen as the mission of the church to take care of these poor people who were out struggling by themselves.

The American Christian Missionary Society (ACMS) reveals this paternalistic attitude in its 1867 minutes which read: "The world is the field, and as in the days of Christ, so now, the harvest truly is great and the laborers are few. At our doors lie the freed men; their bonds broken and their souls open to gentle words and kindly influences.[1]

The main thrust was to do for the Blacks, more so than to do with them. The Anglo-American Disciples provided the schools and the majority of the teachers in them. The Blacks had little or no in-put.

In 1874 Thomas Munnell, corresponding secretary for the ACMS, facilitated the founding of Southern Christian Institute in Edwards, Mississippi, on 160 acres for an elementary school for African-Americans. The ACMS opened the school in 1882 under the leadership of Mrs. Letitia Faurot and her husband, Randall, a former chaplain in the army of Tennessee.

But Robert Hayes Peoples observed that by 1890 Southern Christian Institute faced virtual extinction.

> "The stock company was tired of it. The American Christian Missionary Society did not want it, and there was definite talk about closing It."[2]

C. C. Smith was competing with several other church causes as he tried to raise monies for "Negro work," and was not meeting with success. It was to the credit of ACMS Superintendent J. W. Jenkins that he secured J. B. Lehman to accept its presidency in 1889.

That same year a Board of Negro Education and Evangelism was established in Louisville, Kentucky. C. C. Smith, the White churchman, who had a difficult time trying to administer the ACMS's work among African-Americans since 1867, became its first secretary. Unfortunately, the Board had great difficulty in performance because Smith continued to have trouble securing contributions for this mission work.

Finally in 1900, after the ill-fated attempt to operate a Board of Negro Education and Evangelism, the ACMS turned the Negro mission work over to the Christian Woman's Board of Missions. C. C. Smith, the superintendent of Missions and Schools for Negro Work, had to resign in 1912 because of poor health.

Joel Baer Lehman, then President of Southern Christian Institute in Edwards, Mississippi was appointed his successor. None of this institutional maneuvering was effectively communicated to African-American Disciples leaders. Few were given an opportunity to give input on policy decisions.

Setting up institutions for primary and secondary education, and sending out and supporting a few pastors and state evangelists was the basic strategy of Anglo-American Disciples of Christ for evangelism among Black people.

## THE IMPACT OF JOEL BAER LEHMAN

The impact of Lehman on the nurture and development of the church among African-Americans was tremendous from 1890 through 1922. Almost immediately upon his appointment to succeed C. C. Smith, Lehman launched a campaign to raise $20,000 during the May 1913 Worker's Conference at Southern Christian Institute. It was termed a "jubilee gift for missions"—a celebration of fifty years of freedom and development. Lehman stayed close to the money and to its distribution. As President of Southern Christian Institute and also Superintendent of Negro Work, he commandeered all funds for African-American evangelization and church aid. Further, he impacted the school curriculum not only at Southern Christian Institute, but also at Jarvis Christian Institute, Hawkins, Texas and the other mission schools functioning during his more than thirty years of administration.

Under the administration of African-American church work by the Christian Woman's Board of Missions from 1900 to 1919 and the iron handed administration of J. B. Lehman, the following mission schools either flourished or died: Southern Christian Institute, Edwards, Mississippi (1882); Jarvis Christian Institute, Hawkins, Texas (1914); Piedmont Christian Institute, Martinsville, Virginia (1900); Louisville Bible School, Louisville, Kentucky (1873); Lum Christian Institute, Lum, Alabama; Central Christian Institute, Shepardsville, Kentucky; Goldsboro Christian Institute, Goldsboro, North Carolina; South Carolina Bible Institute, Fairfax, South Carolina; and Tennessee Central Christian Institute, Jonesboro, Tennessee.

Through the Christian Woman's Board of Mission and J. B. Lehman, Black pastors, state and national evangelists like the following were deployed in some eighteen states and given modest stipends of $16.66 to $50 per month.

## TABLE 2

### PASTORS & EVANGELISTS

**PASTORS:**

1. Andrew Jackson Hurdle, Texas
2. Isaiah Quit Hurdle, Texas
3. William Alphin, Texas, Missouri
4. Isaiah H. Moore, Ohio
5. George R. Dorsey, Illinois
6. H.D. Griffin, Washington, DC
7. S.S. Myers, Texas, Oklahoma
8. G.W. Taylor, Texas
9. R. Wesley Watson, Ohio
10. T.W. Giles, Oklahoma
11. S.C. Divine, Ohio
12. J.J. Green, Missouri
13. R.E. LaTouche, Illinois
14. R.H. Davis, Ohio/Illinois

**EVANGELISTS:**

1. H.L. Smith, Texas
2. D.C. Brayboy, Alabama
3. K.R. Brown, Mississippi
4. M.M. Bostick, Arkansas
5. A.J. Jeffries, Alabama
6. W.S. Sims, Kansas
7. P.A. Gray, Missouri
8. B.C. Calvert, Mississippi
9. S.C. Divine, Missouri
10. I.S. Franklin, Mississippi
11. T.W. Giles, Oklahoma

Lehman selected the preachers, determined the length and continuance of their services, and fixed the amount of money they would receive. Meanwhile the evangelists and pastors were expected to raise mission funds from the congregations and report the same to the Superintendent before monthly stipends were received.

## LEHMAN'S IMPACT ON THE SCHOOLS

The manner in which Joel Baer Lehman administered his office of the Superintendent of Negro Work could be called "tight ship administration" by some, but for many Blacks it was regarded as a rampant attitude of paternalism. In the minds of many it reflected the plantation economy mind-set that was so prevalent among many well meaning Anglo-Americans of that day.

No where is Lehman's practice of paternalism more evident than in a review of his relationships with key African-American educators who pioneered in the development of mission schools like Jarvis Christian Institute (College) in Hawkins, Texas. As "superintendent" of all the African-American schools maintained by the Indianapolis based Christian Woman's Board of Missions, he determined budgets, employment of personnel and day-to-day operations.

In this capacity, he was the primary negotiator for purchasing the properties and guiding establishment procedures of Jarvis Christian Institute (College). Yet when he dealt with African-American leadership like the heroic early pioneers T. B. Frost, C. A. Berry and J. N. Ervin, his own files reveal a most demeaning pattern of relationships.

Writing to Major and Mrs. J. Jarvis on June 29, 1912, Lehman states with exuberance: I have just returned from Hawkins and I believe you would be interested in knowing how things are going. Brother and Sister Frost went there at the Holidays and fixed up one cabin for a house and another for a barn. The others had all been carried away before he came. He has fenced about thirty acres around where the sawmill stood on the south side of the railroad and about thirty acres north of the railroad where the cabins were. About twenty acres, south of the railroad, is in corn and truck, and it is the best I saw in that part of Texas.

Brother Frost has arranged with the citizens of Hawkins to make a public road near the railroad to connect Hawkins with Big Sandy. In all I never dreamed he could accomplish so much in such a short time. He seems to have won all the white and colored people to his side.[3]

Yet when Lehman dealt directly with T. B. Frost before Jarvis was placed on the tax free list, he: reprimanded him for paying the taxes before consulting with him; insisted upon giving his approval (or disapproval) of every purchase for the school—even nuts, glassware and a piece of lumber; gave detailed instructions on how Frost should keep the books; and told Mrs. Frost how to take care of their personal money. While C. A. Berry was at Southern Christian Institute in early 1912, J. B. Lehman approached him on the possibility of working at Jarvis. He suggested a salary of $200 a year, and board. C.A. Berry made the following initial response:

While I realize the great work being done among my people by the C.W.B.M., I feel that they might give more than $200 and board. I know we are to sacrifice for this work being done for our own people and do our part and yet I think $240.00 is small enough. $240.00 is much less than I am getting now. I hope you will not think me imposing or trying to get too much salary for the work. I always wanted to do the right thing by the CWBM and feel all concerned will do the same by me.[4]

Of course, President Lehman replied a few days later: "...I know Albert that $200 is not as much as you earn, but Tommy gets only $300 and he has to run the boarding and I did not think it wise to make a disproportion in that way. Another year both of you ought to have salary raised. But to begin with, it is my experience, that if a young man is not willing to make a sacrifice for his people, he will not be a useful worker..."[5]

Mr. Lehman goes on to point out that $200 plus board would be $500 in Jackson, Mississippi, and informs him that he will have to live with the boys in a cabin for a year or two until a new building can be built. The clincher in his pitch to C. A. Berry is: "For the present the plan is to let Brother Frost be the responsible one, but as soon as school is begun Brother Frost understands he is not to be president. I will write you more about this when I hear again.[6]

Later when Lehman informed Berry that Mrs. Atwater of the Christian Woman's Board of Missions had approved his recommendation for Frost to be employed at Jarvis as a staff member, he was told again that he would be given $10 for travel expense and $200 per year plus "free board." Lehman continued: "The plan is now to send some one to the president sometime next year or the year thereafter, but you prove yourself as much better than we expect as Brother Frost has proven himself better than we expected this may not be necessary. Be modest, work hard, and go with a determination to do the very best... and all will come out well...″[7]

Mr. Berry was elated in the knowledge that he had been accepted, but had the audacity to continue questioning of the $200 salary. Eventually he was joined with the Frosts in protest. Berry finally gave in and came to Jarvis. But he continued to appeal for a better salary while working vigorously with T. B. Frost in the construction of buildings and in the improvement of the grounds. Mattie and Thomas Frost joined Berry in the appeal for a better salary. Finally in September of 1913 Lehman promised the Frosts $400 and proceeded to tell Mattie just how she should spend it—even suggesting she might give it back to the institution! (September 1, 1913).

In order to initiate the presence of Jarvis in the Hawkins community, a small grade school was established before the Institute itself was established. By November 12, 1912, Berry and Frost had opened a small school with twenty students. They had classes from the primary grades through the ninth. Their staff and class space was inadequate.

On March 23, 1914, two months after Jarvis Christian Institute was launched, Lehman wrote Frost stating that J. N. Ervin would become the president and that he (Frost) would become the "Superintendent of Industrial Work."

Ervin was a Texan who grew up in Tennessee and was regarded as one of the most refined and respected African-American educators of his day. He was a Latin scholar with a distinguished professional career as a school administrator in Detroit, Michigan, New York City and Johnson City, Tennessee. Beyond his liberal arts degree work he had studied at Columbia University. Yet the manner in which Lehman dealt with him was still paternalistic. He was never treated with the professional courtesies accorded other presidents of institutions of higher education. Ervin, a widower, was advised by Lehman to get married. He was also told where he was to live on campus; given less salary than he was making in Tennessee; and not allowed to employ personnel, buy commodities and equipment, or develop educational programs without the expressed review and endorsement of Lehman.

Soon after Ervin's arrival on the campus as president, Lehman wrote him a four-page letter giving him broad as well as detailed instructions as to how he felt the school should be run. Here are a few excerpts:

"Now Brother Ervin, I want to say a word for Brother and Sister Frost and Brother Berry. After I left you, it occurred to me that I might have left the wrong impression on you in regard to them.... They have grown astonishingly since they went there. To tell you confidentially, I never dreamed that they could do what they did. They opened up the work at a place where a man like you might not have been able to do so. I want to urge upon you to be patient with them, if you should find poor English, and approach them in a helpful spirit..."

Frost left Jarvis November 21, 1921, to establish Central Christian Institute in Shepherdsville, Kentucky. He was pastor of Hill Street Christian Church in Louisville, Kentucky, from 1923-1929 and returned to teach at Southern Christian Institute until he retired on a comfortable home near Hawkins, Texas, in 1939.

Berry remained on the staff at Jarvis as a faculty member. He became a model of excellence for students and faculty. He was to become the father of a distinguished educator and future president of Jarvis Christian College.

But Lehman was not through giving advice to newly employed President J. N. Ervin. He continues: "Now a word about the nature of your courses. This is not in the nature of instructions but simply suggestions. It would be neither wise nor possible for us to think of making a school that would devote itself exclusively to collegiate work. We are building a school that will enable the Negroes of Texas and the other states who may come to your school to become substantial citizens of the country. They must restore the worn out fields, they must build up new enterprises, and they must get homes... I do not feel that you should not work towards a college course, but you should not feel unhappy if the majority of your students will be from the fifth to tenth grade..."

"Now in regard to your boys.... If your boys will come here and will enter into the spirit of our work, we will fit them better for the work they will have to do than would be if they should go thru some of the universities. I urge you to keep your daughter either at Jonesboro, or send her here too..."[8]

Before President Ervin finished his work at Jarvis, he had gained the respect and support of Blacks and many White leaders like L. N. D. Wells, pastor of the leading congregation in Dallas, Texas and W. W. Phares, senior minister of the strong University congregation in Fort Worth.

Before he died, Jarvis became a four-year college, and he was elected the third president of the National Christian Missionary Convention.

## GROWING DISSATISFACTION

The life and works of J. B. Lehman and associates—as noble and necessary as they may have been at the time—depict the socio-religious atmosphere which nurtured seeds of unrest among thoughtful African-American Disciples of Christ.

The move of Black Disciples of Christ to attempt serious organization of the predominantly African-American congregations must be seen against the backdrop of the times. The period of unrest between 1865 to 1900 was for African-Americans what Benjamin Quarles aptly calls "The Decades of Disappointment."[9] The Civil War was over and many Blacks thought that the millennium had come. They rushed forward to take their place on the economic and industrial horizons of the United States. But no sooner than this kind of spirit was manifested by some, the White forces in control of state legislatures instituted the code laws which were designed to "keep the nigger in his place." They restored the old master-slave relationships. Vagrancy laws were instituted and enforced mainly on former slaves who were unable to find employment.

Every aspect of normal living for African-Americans—whether it be preaching, carrying a gun, joining the military, moving freely in public places, or receiving common human services—was controlled by restrictive legislation.

This period of unrest fostered the rise of the Klu Klux Klan and other hate groups. Lynchings and other eruptions of racial violence grew. A struggle for legislative power among Republicans and Democrats ensued. Labor organizations were developed to represent the interests of common workers. All of this was done without due concern for African-Americans. Consequently, the festering climate of anti-African-Americanism continued.

These were also the times when Black and White Disciples of Christ were trying to find ways to work together. Out of the depths of this atmosphere the strong, clear voices of Frederick Douglass, Booker T. Washington, W. E. B. DuBois, and Marcus Garvy could be heard. They called for the African-American people to stand up straight and be the strong citizens the constitution and God intended.

By August 1914, Whites sensed this growing concern. They realized that African-Americans disliked their lives being determined by a predominantly Anglo-American CWBM and the autocratic control of J. B. Lehman. In an attempt to rectify matters, two national workers were appointed. Rosa Brown Bracy became Women's Worker. P. H. Moss was selected by the Christian Woman's Board of Missions to be the Church School and Young People's Worker.

But many of the leaders continued to question the way Lehman was handling "the Negro program". One of the many criticisms was at the point of training leaders for the church. Lehman discouraged higher education for Black church leaders. He was dedicated to the provision of minimum education and the work ethic. This was not necessarily an original idea with him. It seemed to be an adopted stance of the Disciples of Christ before Lehman arrived on the scene.

In the late nineteenth century, when Disciples established the practice of evangelizing African-Americans through schools and deployed evangelists, they were following a path selected by most of the Anglo-American Protestant denominations. There were less than a dozen accredited high schools in the South at the time. There was a scattering of elementary schools, most of which had only from four to six months of school because the children were needed to plant, cultivate, and harvest crops.

The strategy to train Black Disciples of Christ church leaders was largely in the mind of

J. B. Lehman. He felt that if they went through the summer worker's conference he led at Southern Christian Institute, it would suffice.

But while the Disciples were struggling to establish two elementary schools and a high school during the post-Civil War period, African-American denominations were establishing colleges. The African Methodist Episcopal Church established six between 1870-1876. The Colored Methodist Episcopal Church established four between 1878 and 1902. The Freedman's Aid Society of the Methodist church had five colleges and two seminaries by 1878.

The Congregationalists established seven colleges for African-Americans between 1866 and 1869 through their American Missionary Association. Presbyterians had founded Ashnum Institute (later Lincoln University) in 1854. Lehman felt that under his direction, the

Summer Worker's Training Conference at Southern Christian Institute was sufficient.

African-American Disciples leaders were frustrated. This frustration brought about the organization of the National Christian Missionary Convention (NCMC).    They yearned for participation in the administration and implementation of their own affairs.

Two calls went out to Black Disciples of Christ church leaders in 1917 to come together for the formation of an African-American—led and fashioned National Convention. William Alphin gave a call to come to St. Louis during the assembly of the predominantly Anglo-American International Convention. Alphin was a great advocate of cooperation and togetherness between the races. On the other hand, Preston Taylor, W. H. Dickerson, and Henry L. Herod joined in giving a call for the brothers and sisters to come to Nashville, Tennessee, in September 1917. Key leaders answered that call.

## CHAPTER THREE

# LAUNCHING THE SHIP (1900-1917)

The man who has suffered the wrong is the man to demand redress. The man struck is the man to cry out—and the man who has endured the cruel pangs of Slavery is the man to advocate liberty. It is evident that we must be our own representatives and advocates, not exclusively, but peculiarly— not distinct from, but in connection with our white friends.
—*Frederick Douglass, 1851*

There are no figures in the Disciples' YEARBOOK. We claimed six hundred churches, four hundred ministers, fifty percent of which were lay preachers without special charges or training...six schools, one with secondary education, the others elementary, no higher education among Negroes...no newspaper of national import, no general organization or work in which the churches are free to have fellowship in giving to the National work of the church, no leadership for National promotional work other than the Bible... School Secretary put out by the ACMS under the wider auspices of the C.W.B.M.
—*Address of Preston Taylor to first NCMC, 1917*

The leaders of the forty-one persons who gathered in Nashville, Tennessee, on September 5, 1917, were each self-starters and high achievers. Each had lived through slave and/or post-Civil War years roads and climbing steep hills to become mature and refined church leaders in there own right.

In his opening address to the body, Preston Taylor referred to fifty percent of the African-American Disciples of Christ ministers as being lay people with little or no formal training. But this did not characterize those who assumed the leadership of the initial years of the National Christian Missionary Convention. African-Americans in general were struggling for a place of significance on the United States scene. Among these Disciples attending the first National Convention were the following:

(a)     Preston Taylor was born a slave November 7, 1849 in Shreveport, Louisiana. In 1888 he purchased his first 37 acres to establish Greenwood Cemetery in Nashville, Tennessee. Later he expanded it with 33.3 additional acres; established the first recreational park for Blacks in the South; and managed a successful mortician's business, all while being pastor of Nashville's prestigious Lea Avenue Christian Church. He would leave a large portion of his estate to African-American Disciples of Christ and the Christian Church in general.

(b)     William Alphin, who issued the parallel "call" to assemble, had attended Lemoyne Owen College in Memphis, Tennessee, and engaged in a noteworthy ministry in Texas as a pastor and state evangelist. He would be chosen to make the first draft of the National Convention's Constitution as well as become its third vice-president.

(c)     The W. H. and C. H. Dickerson  brothers were both brilliant churchmen.
        W. H. was a professor in Crofton, Kentucky and C. H. was a gifted pastor and poet from Lexington, Kentucky. Both would take their places in Convention  leadership; W. H. Dickerson to be a second vice-president and C. H. Dickerson to serve on the first "Advisory Committee to the White People in Their Work Among Negroes."

(d)     Dr. J. E. Walker was the first treasurer. He graduated from medical school as a doctor, established a successful insurance company and was an ardent and committed church lay leader. He would be the Convention's treasurer for forty years.

(e)     Henry L. Herod had been schooled at Butler University and the University of Chicago. He had laid the foundation for the widely known Flanner Settlement House in

Indianapolis, Indiana, and continued to serve as its director while performing with excellence as pastor of Second Christian Church. He would become the Convention's first secretary.

(f)     R. E. Pearson with professorial credentials and great tendencies toward philosophizing and oratory, had met success as a pastor in Kentucky and would become the corresponding secretary.

(g)     Sarah Lue Bostic, born May 27, 1868 near Glasgow, Kentucky, under lowly circumstances, had been ordained to ministry in the Disciples of Christ on April 24, 1892. By 1917, the time of Taylor's call, she had been an outstanding field worker for the Christian Woman's Board of Mission since 1899 and would give a stirring message to this first gathering just before they would vote to organize the National Christian Missionary Convention.  She would continue to serve the church for forty years.

This is only a sample listing of the distinguished group of forty-one persons which makes no reference to the P. H. Moss's, W. A. Scott's, T. R. Everett's, Sarah Blackburn's, Rosa V. Brown's, Henry L. Herod's., and W. P. Martin's.

One must quickly dispel the notion that the founders of the National Christian Missionary Convention were unlearned neophytes striving for a place in the sun.  Most had already made a high mark for the Lord.  Most agreed with the thinking of Frederick Douglass who believed "that we must be our own representatives and advocates, not exclusively, but peculiarly—not distinct from, but in connection with our Anglo-American friends."

## A TIME OF SOCIAL FERMENTATION

Thus, at a time when race relations in America were tense, and when the blood of African-Americans and some Anglo-Americans was being shed daily because of racial discord, Black Disciples of Christ leadership was advocating a path of racial cooperation. They wanted to walk alongside their Anglo-American brothers and sisters as partners in Christian mission. This was possibly the most unique historical aspect of the founding of the National Christian Missionary Convention!

So among the forty-one persons invited and attending the first assemblage of the National Christian Missionary Convention were a number of White Disciples of Christ. However, available church records do not fully reflect their awareness of the momentous time that they had chosen to call a national church meeting. It was an hour in society fraught with sociological explosives. The recorded words and actions of the Anglo-Americans during the Nashville meeting do not indicate any comprehension of the impact racial tension as a whole was having on the attitudes and aspirations on African-American Disciples of Christ leadership.

On April 6, 1917 the United States had entered World War I. President Wilson, who had promised African-Americans a fair deal, was quietly instituting Jim Crow laws in government while urging Congress to win a war because "the world must be safe for democracy."[1]

Less than a month (July 1-3) before Disciples of Christ assembled in Nashville, Tennessee, some forty to two hundred persons had been killed in an East St. Louis, Illinois, race riot. Less than a week before Preston Taylor gave the opening address, some ten thousand Blacks had marched down Fifth Avenue in New York City protesting race lynchings and other miscarriages of justice.

Against the background of these happenings, approximately a decade before (July 11-13, 1905), W.E.B. Du Bois had quietly gathered a select group of intellectuals and activists in the Niagara Falls African-American strategy conference on how to secure human freedom.

Later, W. E. B. Du Bois, plus much of the work done by attendees at the Niagara Conference, would become part of the NAACP. On the 100th anniversary of Abraham Lincoln's birthday (February 9,1909) forty-seven Anglo-Americans and six African-Americans founded the National Association for the Advancement of Colored People. It was Du Bois who shaped its early thought and much of its strategy from his editorship of the NAACP journal called THE CRISIS.[2]

While the Christian Woman's Board of Mission was appointing P. H. Moss and Rosa Brown Bracy as national field workers for Black Disciples of Christ congregations in 1914, the Ku Klux Klan was becoming rooted in Fulton County, Georgia. By 1915 it spread like a cancer throughout the South, Midwest (especially Indiana and Ohio) and the West.

In the light of these tempestuous times, what the Black Disciples of Christ said to those attending the first National Christian Missionary

Convention was indeed restrained. Taylor possibly made the most biting remarks. He criticized Whites for being half-hearted in their approach to the evangelization and cultivation of African-Americans. He deplored the non-committal stance of White Disciples on race, which he said was the reason for the smallness of Black Disciples numbers. Taylor regretted the lack of an effective means for inter-communication among African-American Disciples of Christ. Yet he appealed for greater cooperation between the races in "building the kingdom of God." He pled for a better program for producing adequately prepared ministerial leaders.

R. E. Pearson stressed the need for an organizational vehicle led by African-Americans, which would provide an arena for meaningful dialogue and interaction with predominantly Anglo-American-led church structures. Others like W. A.   Scott of Jackson, Mississippi; Sarah Bostic of Little Rock, Arkansas; Sarah Blackburn of Port Gibson, Mississippi gave theological and practical reasons for cooperation in doing the Lord's work.  Scott felt that even as the Father, Son and Holy Spirit were a cooperating unit, so must the church be such a body. And Bostic and Blackburn, who were effective representatives of the Christian Woman's Board of Missions, lifted up CWBM as a model of how cooperative effort could be advanced. But on the whole, the Anglo-American representatives made cautious statements. Almost none gave whole-hearted endorsement for an African-America-led national convention. Most supported the idea of cooperation to be advanced through existing structures.

An impressive number of Disciples national agencies were already in place. The following is a listing of some:

### TABLE 3

AMERICAN CHRISTIAN MISSIONARY SOCIETY
(1849-1919)

CHRISTIAN WOMAN'S BOARD OF MISSION
(1874-1919)

FOREIGN CHRISTIAN MISSIONARY SOCIETY
(1875-1919)

NATIONAL BENEVOLENT ASSOCIATION
(1886-Present)

## BOARD OF CHURCH EXTENSION
### (1888-Present)

## BOARD OF EDUCATION
### (1894-Present)

## BOARD OF MINISTERIAL RELIEF
### (1895-Present)

This same year, 1917, the International Convention of Disciples of Christ itself was struggling to be born.[3] It is quite possible that pastors of predominantly Anglo-American congregations as well as the executives of agencies like the above were overloaded with organizational meetings. Disciples were threatened with a multiplicity of agencies and societies. Discussions were already underway as to how the American Christian Missionary Society, the Christian Woman's Board of Mission, and the Foreign Christian Missionary Society could unite their work. Somost Anglo-American Disciples of Christ agency leaders were lukewarm toward the African-American desire to organize another national structure.

During this first Convention the Secretary of the Foreign Christian Missionary Society, Stephen J. Cory, attended and led a round-table on how his agency related to African-Americans. Mrs. Atwater, Secretary for the Christian Woman's Board of Mission, was there to point out Black Disciples' deficiencies in Christian stewardship. She then made a presentation of Jacob Kenoly, whom Afro-Americans had sent as a missionary to Jerusalem in the mid-nineteenth century by the American Christian Missionary Society.

Robert M. Hopkins, the National Sunday School secretary, held a round-table discussion on how his office functioned, especially with the help of recently employed Patrick H. Moss who was assigned to Black congregations. Joel Baer Lehman's involvement as a round-table leader brought the most negative response. He tried to play down the importance of focusing on racial self-development and the attainment of excellence in education. According to the minutes "the brethren then put rapid questions to Brother Lehman of great import."

On Thursday afternoon, September 7, 1917, the body voted that "this congress dissolve into a regular National or General Convention of Colored Churches of Christ." The first meeting climaxed with the adoption of a resolution to form a vehicle by which future program and services could be done cooperatively through the appointment of an "Advisory Committee to the White People in Their Work Among Negroes." The resolution read: "The National Christian Woman's Board of Missions, having granted through its representatives to the Colored National Convention, the privilege of appointing a committee of five persons to be   chosen from its members, as representatives to confer with that body about the work to be done by it in and among the Negroes of the Christian Church, the following are appointed: Preston Taylor,  H.L. Herod, Ross V. Brown, C. H. Dickerson, and W. W. Cordell."[4]

Considering the highly charged secular atmosphere between the races in the United States at the time of the Nashville meeting, it may be considered quite remarkable that the meeting was held at all. James Blair, in trying to summarize the reasons for the formulation of the National Christian Missionary Convention, made the following observations:[5]

* The need for a good institution of higher education which would provide quality education for Black people;

* Treatment of second-class Christian citizenship which seemed to permeate most relationships between Blacks and Whites in the church;

* Lack of public accommodations being available to Blacks when they attended large gatherings of White members of the Christian Churches and no strong advocacy by the White Convention for the securing of such accommodations for all attendants regardless of race;

* Lack of communication between the church bureaucracy serving Blacks and an unwritten policy that Blacks "were being told what was best for them, rather than being asked what was best;" * Need for communication and understanding among Black Disciples themselves;

* Need for an elimination of stereotype ideas about race through the creative interaction of competent Blacks and Whites.

Blair concluded that the first gathering of the National Christian Missionary Convention was the means by which the Brotherhood was shocked into the awareness that the Negro had changed. He had changed from Uncle Tom to "Mr. Thomas" and had to be encountered in a different way. This conclave also showed the Negro that there was concern for the Negro work and that the Negroes were not doing all they could to promote the work of the total brotherhood, and that white people cannot be thought of in general terms; they had to be thought of as individuals. All of them were not hate-ridden and scheming to keep the Negro down...[6]

Black Disciples of Christ in the company of both willing and hesitant Whites had taken one small step toward the kingdom of God in the midst of very troubled times.

## CHAPTER FOUR

# REFINING OBJECTIVES (1917 - 1920)

To make the world safe for democracy there must be a new system of education and this new system must be granted to all peoples and races and the Bible must be the central force in it; for no individual, race or nation will be safe for the principles of democracy until that individual, race or nation knows God.
—*Richard H. Davis, Pastor, Cincinnati, Ohio On Education for Democracy at 1918 NCMC*

...this democracy must be all-inclusive. She must hover all men beneath her protective wings. If any are to be denied, the blessed boon of her loving care, they must be excluded as individuals and never as groups... She must know neither male nor female, black nor white, Jew nor Greek... On the one hand, the reach of her wing must equal the fatherhood of God; on the other, the brotherhood of man.
—*James H. Thomas, President of Piedmont Christian Institute on "Making the World Safe for Democracy" at 1918 NCMC*

The second annual meeting of the National Christian Missionary Convention had a theme very much in keeping with the turbulent times—MAKING THE WORLD SAFE FOR DEMOCRACY. Addresses to the 1918 convention, like one given by James H. Thomas of Martinsville, Virginia, and related forums on the operation of the Christian Church, gave honest consideration to the challenging subject. For, indeed, what African-American Disciples of Christ wanted most was the Christian Church to be a biblically based model of a true democratic community. But for the next five Conventions the body spent most of its time on internal matters while the issues of program services to the congregations was handled mainly by a small select joint committee of appointees from the Convention, and the chief Anglo-American agency executives in Indianapolis, Indiana.

Anglo-American staff attending the Convention during these years seized the opportunity to do financial promotion. Following apologies for not working more closely with the predominantly Black congregations, Convention attendees were often challenged to improve what was termed their small contributions to the cooperative work.

While Lehman's reports continued to reflect the separation between the races at the congregational and state levels, he contended that Anglo-Americans in many instances were being supportive of what was being done in the Black churches. Most state evangelists like K. R. Brown in Mississippi, and W. H. Dickerson in Ohio reported good cooperation with existing African-American church organizations but no contacts at all with their Anglo-American counterparts.

Nevertheless, cooperation remained a central objective of Convention leadership. William Alphin who helped make the original draft of the Constitution was a strong advocate of this principle. A 1919 refinement of the document included the following statement of policy:

> Cooperation with other organizations of Disciples or otherwise shall not be denied. The wisdom and nature of such cooperation, when not expressed by the Convention, shall be left to the wisdom of the Executive Committee.[1]

The press for "cooperation" between Conventions in the National Christian Missionary Convention was so strong that at the 1920 Convention, which met August 31 though September 5, a newly formed Commission on Organic Operative Relations Between the National Convention of Churches of Christ and the International Convention issued the following challenge:

> We recommend, pursuant to the request of the recent conferences of the advisory committees of this Convention and the Executive Committee of the C.W.B.M. that a committee of two be elected to cooperate with a like number chosen from the International Convention to study the question of organic and operative relations between the two bodies and to report findings and recommendations to the respective bodies in 1921.[2]

This quest for establishing some kind of an official relationship to the International Convention became a continuing agenda item for Disciples of Christ.

## DEFINING THE CONVENTION'S ROLE AND OBJECTIVES

When James H. Thomas addressed the 1921 Convention on the PURPOSE AND SCOPE OF THE NATIONAL CONVENTION, James Blair aptly termed it a "Declaration and Address of the Negro Disciples of Christ." (See Appendix for fuller text.) Thomas, the founder and President of Piedmont Christian Institute, Martinsville, Virginia, had been unable to attend the first meeting of the Convention. However, his address indicates he had given careful study to why the convention was necessary.

With an eloquence most characteristic of public speakers from the South in that day, Thomas pointed to: (a) "race antipathy" which contributed to voluntary and enforced segregation; (b) the need for a forum where there could be "free interchanging of views and the impartation of ideas... irrespective of race...;" (c) the fostering of programs that tap the "vast and undeveloped resources" of African-Americans in the Church of Christ; and (d) the persistent need for the larger vision as the main reasons for establishing a national convention for African-American Disciples of Christ. Thomas maintained that:

> The aim and purpose of this Convention is to set before all the larger vision; to provide us with a truer, more accurate estimate of our resources and strength; and so inspire us with the determination to have a worthier share in the furtherance of the church as a whole. Small as we are, admittedly in comparison of    other Negro religious communions, we are still a little giant, did we but know it, and as we would surely discover if once we could be induced to put forth the best that is in us in the accomplishment of some worthy task.[3]

Thomas saw the National Convention and the general church body as being joined together in one over-arching Christian mission, generated by the Holy Spirit, which comes from one Lord, one faith and one baptism. Thomas did not see a national convention duplicating program services, which could be better, secured through existing agencies and staffs.

President Taylor looked back over the first four years and had an optimistic view of the future. His opening address referred to the humble beginning made by Herod, Dickerson and himself when they first met under a tree in Greenwood Park of Nashville, Tennessee. They fashioned the call for the first meeting. He called it "the greatest project a united church has ever undertaken." He noted that "sixteen states were well represented in the beginning of the organization" and that larger and better plans had been made for each annual meeting that followed.  With the flair of the preacher, he proclaimed "...now we stand on the fourth rung of the ladder that we are building and lengthening toward the eternal shores beyond."[4]

However, the debate as to what the nature and program of the National Christian Missionary Convention should be mounted a low intensity during the early 1920's.  The chief medium for communication was THE GOSPEL PLEA, which was published in Edwards, Mississippi. It was edited and controlled by J. B. Lehman. He was still president of Southern Christian Institute, and Superintendent of Educational and Evangelistic Work for Negroes. In the July 1, 1922 issue of THE GOSPEL PLEA [5], some of the aspects of that debate are revealed. Lehman used an editorial entitled, "Can We Work the Program?" to attack a position William Alphin set forth in an article called "The National Convention". Alphin was pointing toward the fifth annual meeting of the convention to be held in Indianapolis, Indiana. "To be a constructive convention, Alphin declared, it must be more of a Negro convention.... I do not mean to exclude the White people from our meetings or having places on our programs... I do mean a Negro convention  with a program consisting largely of Negroes, and suggesting methods and work for Negro churches from the Negroes viewpoint.... I think our conventions have failed to be more constructive and influential with the pastors and local churches because their methods and plans miss   the mark.... I think the color of face has something to do with it. If the Emergency Campaign had been workable for our churches, most of us would have stood by it and put it over.... But we voted "yes" in their presence and disappointed them in their absence. I firmly believe we ought to strive...to redeem ourselves along financial lines to Indianapolis.[6]

Alphin concluded by urging the brothers and sisters to come to the Indianapolis convention prepared to have a "Negro convention but no less a convention of fellowship in the larger work," and to "work to make the Convention a money-raising convention...." "The money, brethren, will solve all the real and imaginary problems we are having with the UCMS (i. e United Christian Missionary Society which came into being in 1919 and inherited the responsibility for administering services to African-American congregations).

Alphin's article was on page three and Lehman countered with a front-page editorial with the headline: A SURVEY. The Superintendent contended:

> The Disciples of Christ who have earnestly contended for unity on first principles are determined that there shall be no division on race and color. Any other position would mean that we must have one denomination of the White Christians, another of Japanese Christians, another of Chinese Christians, another of Hindu Christians, another of Negro Christians, and so on...

> But when it comes to heading up the work in our great missionary   enterprises and in our International Convention, we must be one or make separate denominations. In order to accomplish this the White secretaries are taking full part in Negro conventions, and the Negro convention is given representation on the Recommendations Committee...

> All the true leaders from Frederick Douglass, through Paul Lawrence Dunbar, to Booker T. Washington the White people have helped to make them. And vice versa, there will be no true leaders of White people made from now on unless the Negroes help make them... The whole contention of Brother Alphin is diametrically opposed to all we are doing, not only in the church, but in a sociological way...[7]

Lehman went on to declare "We are trying to put away the ten foot pole and teach handshake." He made a strong case for continuing interaction between the races. Then, thinking about the UCMS budget he administered for aiding in African-American church development, he made the prediction that "we can in a few years raise our budget to $200,000 annually and we can put to work every worthy Negro man and woman."

During the fifth annual meeting of the NCMC in Indianapolis, Indiana, Patrick Henry Moss, the Black Sunday School field staff, underscored the point-of-view William Alphin was trying to advance. The highly respected Moss declared:

"The present standard course is pretty stiff, and requires uncommon ability to teach it. I realize that an ideal standard will and would cause one to strive but I am wondering if these standards are prepared with the common people in mind. If these writers could only spend a few months among the schools in the open country and small towns it would help them to understand the needs, and thus prepare an elementary course which is not too rigid, for their education is too limited."

Moss was the national field staff who conducted training institutes; established new Sunday schools and revived old ones; standardized church schools; held schools of methods; and conducted various kinds of group conferences. His field experience among Blacks was extensive. The refinement of Convention objectives and attempts to establish meaningful relationships with the International Convention of the Christian Church would continue to be a major part of NCMC annual agendas.

## NEW DIRECTIONS IN ADMINISTRATION

In 1919, the American Christian Missionary Society, Foreign Christian Missionary Society, Board of Temperance and Social Welfare, and Christian Woman's Board of Mission merged into the United Christian Missionary Society. The Department of Home Missions basically inherited C.W.B.M's responsibility for administering program services to Black congregations.

The Advisory Committee to Whites and later the Joint Executive Committee with J. B. Lehman as chairman, continued to exert considerable influence on the direction of program services up through the years of the Great Economic Depression. The Joint Committee, working through the UCMS framework and having some accountability to the Convention, changed the administrative style of J. B. Lehman from what had been essentially an autocratic style to a consultative one.

From the early nineteenth century, when Disciples of Christ met in districts and states for the purpose of "cooperation", to the founding of the ACMS in 1849, and the International Convention in 1917, the desire was to link the big meeting to the needs of the churches and receive financial support from both individuals and congregations. The founding of the National Christian Missionary Convention was faced with the same challenges in 1917. So at its very inception arrangements were made to tie its existence to the lifeblood and interests of congregations.

Convention leadership gave high priority to developing workable relationships for program services and monitoring the work of the embryonic national African-American staff. In the beginning that meant J. B. Lehman, superintendent, Edwards, Mississippi; Rosa Grubbs, field secretary for Women's Mission, St. Louis, Missouri; Patrick Henry Moss, Secretary of Bible School and Deetsey Blackburn, Elementary Superintendent, both of Kansas City, Kansas.

On the other hand, concern for developing relationships with the International Convention and similar structures was significant if it enhanced the possibility for improved services to Black congregations. Later these goals were to broaden into a larger world view.

The Convention helped in the delivery of program services to Blacks by attempting to provide from $10,000 to $20,000 of UCMS budget for such services. It also appointed from five to seven members of the Joint Executive Committee, which aided the Superintendent of Negro Education and Evangelism to administer the program. The President of the National Convention was given automatic membership.

This committee: (a) developed the convention budget; (b) approved convention program; (c) promoted financial stewardship; (d) reviewed the staff schedules for field visitations; (e) received reports on the financial status of the mission schools; (f) approved staff employment and salaries; (g) established and administered the publication of a national paper; and (h) received and reviewed the reports of field workers.

From 1920 through 1930 the Convention, working through the Joint Executive Committee, challenged the Black congregations to support such activities as the following:

* the Emergency Fund campaign with Rosa Grubbs as director;

* publication of THE CHRISTIAN PLEA and employment of Prince A. Gray, Jr. and Vance Smith as editors;

* children and youth work through Elementary Superintendents Deetsey Blackburn Gray, Bessie Chandler, and Secretary of Religious Education Patrick Henry Moss;

* continuation of mission support of fifteen to twenty pastors and evangelists in twelve states; and encouragement of students and financial support for:

   -Southern Christian Institute, Edwards, Mississippi

   -Jarvis Christian Institute, Hawkins, Texas

   -Piedmont Christian Institute, Martinsville, Virginia

   -Alabama Christian Institute, Lum, Alabama

   -Central Christian Institute, Shepherdsville, Kentucky.

President Lehman, the long-term superintendent of Negro missions, gave evidence of growth in his comprehension of what Black Disciples of Christ wanted, and to some degree, needed. On December 7, 1928, in an effort to get some idea of what comparable denominations were doing in African-American church development, he wrote Bishop Theodore D. Bratton of the Episcopal Diocese of Mississippi:

1. How much do the Episcopalians spend annually for Negro education and evangelization?

2. How many schools do they maintain?

3. Is the field work education and evangelization done entirely by Negroes or do you have some White workers?

The bishop replied with breakdowns indicating that Episcopalians gave $441,795 for nine African-American institute schools and $230,935 for evangelization in twenty-two dioceses. He ended by saying "as quickly as we can we train Negroes for the work."[8]

The economic turn down initiated by the stock market crash of 1929 caused a diminishing number of students and finance which eventually required the closing of Piedmont in 1932, Alabama (Lum) in 1923, and Central in 1923.

## NCMC: MODUS OPERANDI FOR MISSION

During the first decade of the National Convention's existence it had worked with concerned Anglo-American Disciples leaders in fashioning relationships for the delivery of national agency program services to predominantly African-American congregations.

* The Joint Executive Committee, with an equal number of members from the NCMC and the United Christian Missionary Society, was given over-all review, evaluation and confirmation.

* Predominantly African-American state and regional church structures and cooperative pastors and congregations were open for the visitation and presentations of national Black staff. Black staff was given field assignments to Black church groups which had been independently organized in Illinois, Missouri, Tennessee, Kentucky, Kansas, Maryland, Oklahoma, Ohio, Mississippi, Virginia, South Carolina, North Carolina, West Virginia, Florida, District of Columbia, Alabama, Arkansas, Georgia, and Indiana.

* Input to the formation of general church priorities and policy could come through NCMC representation on the recommendation committee of the International Convention. As early as 1919 an NCMC International Committee proposed sending an official representative to the Convention to be held in St. Louis, and further suggested that the various boards affiliated with the International Convention consider the appointment of an African-American board member and each employ African-American staff. During the fifth National Convention which met at Jarvis, August 23-28, 1921, Preston Taylor and Mrs. Hattie Singleton were elected to represent the Convention on the Recommendations Committee of the International Convention which met in Winona Lake, Wisconsin, the following week. The following year Taylor and Singleton reported to the National Convention that they had been given all of the appropriate courtesies and "were assigned to one of the most important committees where we rendered very satisfactory service...".

* The National Convention was presented an "asking budget" which ranged from $10,000 to $12,000. This was a little more than half of the approximately $17,000 to $19,500 needed by the United Christian Missionary Society in the early years to provide staff services for Black people. A high amount of $10,106.15 was collected from the field in 1924-25. But in 1929-30, as the nation's economy worsened, the National Convention could only muster $6,255.62.

* The annual meeting of the Convention, therefore, became the major arena for the accounting of mission stewardship and the evaluation and confirmation of activities in Christian witness. The

early years saw the meetings scheduled mainly in the mid-south: Nashville, Tennessee; Paducah, Kentucky; and Hawkins, Texas. Then in the last half of the first decade they moved mid-west and east to Indianapolis, Indiana; Kansas City, Missouri; Chicago, Illinois; Cincinnati, Ohio; Louisville, Kentucky and Washington, D. C.

* NCMC also had a direct relationship to the welfare of the mission schools by allowing representatives to appear at the annual assemblies for recruitment presentations, and to respond to direct appeals for financial assistance beyond that received through UCMS.

* Key to the coordination and execution of the process was the executive staff person under the employee of the UCMS. J. B. Lehman had set the precedent on how that office should function. Through the years he, too, broadened in his comprehension of the vision and task.

## CHAPTER FIVE

# IMPLEMENTING THE VISION (1920-1930)

## ACHIEVING THE EDUCATIONAL ASPECTS OF THE VISION

The National Convention leadership joined in the struggle for quality education from the very outset. Lay education as well as adequate ministerial preparation was an announced priority in 1917 by its founder, Preston Taylor. In the face of the racial riots and lynchings which happened in each of the early years of the Convention's existence, the founders were mindful of the early attempts of various individuals and groups which sought to improve opportunities for African-Americans to receive quality education.

In his opening address to the 1917 Convention, Taylor said: "The question of leadership among any people is always vital, particularly is this true of the colored people. Increased difficulty here should be met with increased ability, not less ability. Moreover, the churches of large experience in this field, have all except our own recognized this fact..."[1]

Examples of what Preston Taylor had in mind were the Presbyterians and their establishment of Lincoln University as Ashmond Institute in Chester, Pennsylvania, in 1854; the African Methodist Episcopal Church and their founding of Wilberforce University in Wilberforce, Ohio, in 1856; the Congregationalists and their starting of Fisk University in Nashville, Tennessee, and the Baptists Shaw University in Raleigh, North Carolina, in 1865, following again in 1867 with the establishment of Morehouse College in Atlanta, Georgia. Taylor continued in his address:

"Finally, the colored brethren have no future without able leadership. Some of us doubt if they seriously believe in it. It is to be remembered that it is extremely difficult, if not quite impossible, to make first class leaders by third rate methods. We are in dire need of at least one school of standard college curriculum where our leaders, especially those entering the ministry, may be adequately equipped for their work; where the boys and girls of the church may have a liberal education in the church; where they may be won for Christian leadership..."[2]

Through membership on the Joint Executive Committee of the UCMS Convention leaders gave advice and counsel on a strategy. They gave priority for youth conferences to provide the atmosphere for the education and recruitment of youth for church vocations. The first of these conferences was held at Southern Christian Institute, Edwards, Mississippi in 1928.

## THE YOUTH CONFERENCE

The conference lasted for a week and had as its purpose the intellectual, physical, social, and spiritual development of young people. Courses were offered in "Training for Leadership", "The Origin and Nature of the Bible", "Vocational Guidance", "Story Telling", and "The Task of the Church." During the day and following the vesper service there was opportunity for informal conversation with adult faculty and counselors and some form of supervised recreation. There were times for games, singing and wholesome socializing.

Spiritual development was enhanced by a "Morning Watch". This was the time when conferees went to some secluded spot with their Bibles for meditation and engagement in prayer. The climax of the day was the closing friendship circle, which was conducted, in a simple but impressive fashion. Then there was silence and bed.

On the final evening of the conference, the friendship circle was preceded by communion and was a time when conferees could make a commitment and dedication to full-time Christian service. It was one of the major sources of recruitment to Christian ministry in the Black church.

A similar conference movement developed among the predominantly Anglo-American states and areas. But for African-Americans in the early years of racial separatism, the Convention encouraged the summer conference idea to spread from the Magnolia (SCI) Conference in Edwards, Mississippi to the Midwest at Bonner Springs, Kansas; Southwest at Jarvis Christian College in Hawkins, Texas; Alabama, Central Kentucky; and Piedmont Tri-State District in Martinsville, Virginia.

Patrick H. Moss and Vance Smith gave early guidance to the youth conference movement. But in 1935 Robert Hayes Peoples became the first African-American Secretary of all African-American church work and eventually became known as "the daddy" of all the conference deans. In this capacity he touched and guided many young men and women into Christian Church leadership.

## EDUCATION OF THE LAITY

The Convention's direct involvement in achieving some of the educational aspects of the vision was expanded beyond Sunday school to the whole field of religious education and leader development. During the first decade of the Convention, the original staff of Grubbs, Moss, Blackburn and Lehman was expanded with the addition of William Alphin and Vance Smith.

Daisy June Trout, Executive for Women and Missions, joined J. B. Lehman in the oversight of itineraries. The staff attended every state meeting and sometimes included a town-by-town visitation of congregations, leading up to and surrounding a state meeting. In each situation they were expected to do some teaching.

A key teaching model for the field visitation was termed the "United Society One-Day Convention". One model called for an emphasis on "definite giving.@ The program called for the entire staff to meet on a Saturday at approximately 10:30 am and continue until 8:30 pm. An agenda called for devotions; survey of the field locally, nationally and world wide; a message from the "missionary"; a presentation on "how to give;" review of literature; adjournment for a two-hour lunch period; a four and-a-half-hour afternoon session which covered the organized cooperative work; the National Convention budget; THE CHRISTIAN PLEA; release of "quotas" and packets; simultaneous conferences for men and women; and an optional religious education conference.

The one-day conference closed out with a two-hour session after dinner, which covered devotions by the "team leader", a series of brief messages by general field secretaries, a talk by the "missionary," and an "illustrated lecture" on "Our World Wide Work".

The Convention, in cooperation with the United Christian Missionary Society, was providing direct staff services to African-American Disciples of Christ church workers. These services were not available to them from state church organizations where they resided.

On December 22, 1926, the Joint Executive Committee approved of a plan for the publication of THE CHRISTIAN PLEA in cooperation with Christian Board of Publication and designated Vance Smith as editor. They proposed that he live in one of the mission rooms of the Society, be paid $100 per month and devote three-fourths of his time to the paper and one-fourth to the Department of Religious Education. African-American Disciples had long wanted a journal, which they felt they controlled. This proposal eventually went through, but only after long debate in the tenth annual meeting of the Convention in Louisville, Kentucky. THE CHRISTIAN PLEA became another means of general education.

There were remarkable historic events, which affected African-Americans during these years of the 1930s, and the Great Economic Depression. There were the beginnings of the NAACP to make a legalistic onslaught on racial segregation in higher education (1933), and the rise of Joe Louis (1937) and Jesse Owens (1936) as images of African-American achievement. In the face of the Daughters of the American Revolution's refusal of Marian Anderson to use Constitutional Hall for a musical, there was her dramatic Easter Sunday concert before 75,000 African-Americans and Anglo-Americans amassed on the steps of Lincoln Monument in Washington, D.C. (1939). But few records reflect the interest of African-American Disciples of Christ in society as Christian citizens.

## EXPANSION TO MINISTERS

Soon after R. H. Peoples became the National Secretary of Negro work, and was joined by Carnella Jamison (now Barnes) as the Field Secretary for Women's Work, he developed the Regional Church Workers Institute. The program offered courses in developing congregational program and included seminars on church problems.

The needs of ministers were included through courses on pastoral work, preaching, the life and teachings of Jesus, and church administration. Institutes were held from 1936 to 1940 in Kentucky, Tennessee, Texas, Illinois, Indiana and Ohio. Eventually the annual meeting of the National Convention became the major place for religious education for all age levels and fellowship groups.

With the addition of C. L. Parks and Charles H. Webb who became Field Directors for Membership and Evangelism, the model of the Minister's Institute was introduced. Then when Lorenzo Evans became Director of Christian education, he seconded Bessie E. Chandler to assist in establishing laboratory schools for teacher training in 1950 and eventually the very successful School of Faith and Life in 1965. These became an established part of the annual assembly of the National Christian Missionary Convention.

But the major focus remained the minister's ability to secure adequate training in existing church-sponsored institutions of higher education. The annual meeting of the National Convention provided an arena for advocates of improved higher education to be heard and to provoke discussion. Sometimes those presentations brought creative responses.  During the fourth assembly of the National Convention, which was held in Paducah, Kentucky, August 21-27, 1920, C. W. Smith, dean of Jarvis Christian Institute, lifted up the need for well-prepared ministerial leadership who could serve Blacks who were migrating to the growing urban areas. Stressing the need for high quality curriculum and instructional performance in mission schools, he said:

> "My idea is that the courses in our schools, whether Bible, literary or industrial ought to be taught sufficiently thorough that when the student completes a course in our schools he will be able to compete with the practical workers of the world. For example, ... do not say we are teaching shoe-making when we have one little class and no instructor. Do not claim to be teaching printing when our own little job work must be sent elsewhere to be done; do not claim to be teaching modern laundering when we still use the old battling stick and wash kettle method, a method used by our great grandmothers; do not claim to teach scientific agriculture when the most ordinary farmer can beat us getting results. My contention is that if we claim to offer certain courses it ought to be so."

"I believe that the time has come when our churches and schools must establish businesses in connection with them for their maintenance. Our churches and schools moved along slowly because they have been beggars instead of business institutions."[3]

Such presentations in the assemblies of the National Convention brought spirited discussion. But they moved along the stream of progress. Within the first ten years of the life of Jarvis, J. Ervin was encouraged to raise the institution from an elementary school in 1914 to be recognized by the state Department of Education of Texas as a high school in 1924. Three years later it became a junior college. In 1938 President Peter C. Washington succeeded Ervin who was in failing health. Under Washington's leadership Jarvis was placed on the accredited list as a senior college by the Texas State Department of Education in 1941. By 1947, following the increase in the number of volumes of books in the library and the up-grading of faculty, Jarvis was recognized as an accredited four-year college by the Southern Association of Colleges and Secondary Schools.[4]

In 1939 Charles Berry and E. W. Rand produced a study on "Negro Education in the Disciple Brotherhood" which stated, "...the responsibility of the college, and particularly the church-related college, is to assume the roll of leadership in resolving the conflicts, if we are to attain the maximum adjustments in peace, goodwill and fraternity, before the time limits."[5]

Berry and Rand were concerned about the extent to which the Disciples of Christ "perpetuate the ideals of freedom, justice and dignity of the individual by offering to its Negro youth an educational program comparable to that of White youth".[6]

The National Convention provided UCMS staff a receptive arena where research findings on the needs of ministers could be reported and suggestions given for action. R. H. Peoples was prompted to study the status of African-American ministry in twenty-three states from 1934 to 1939. He studied 186 predominantly African-American congregations served by 140 ministers. One hundred and seven churches were rural and seventy-nine classified as urban.

But out of the 140 ministers only three had attended a seminary, and two had done graduate work. Seventy-four, or more than half of them (52.8%), had less than a high school education. Ten had finished high school and twenty-nine had completed college work.

The Peoples' study showed that out of the twenty-six institutions cooperating with the Disciples of Christ Board of Higher Education, eighteen had programs for the training of ministers. Of these eighteen church-affiliated institutions four—Drake University, Eureka College, Chapman College and Butler University—were the only ones who would admit African-Americans.

The study findings were discussed widely by persons attending the National Convention as well as staff in Indianapolis. Merle R. Eppse, the Black professor of history at Tennessee A. and I. State College in Nashville, Tennessee, succeeded C. H. Dickerson as editor of THE CHRISTIAN PLEA. He gave liberal space and editorial comment in the publication.

The response of the Convention came through: a) the establishment of the Taylor Co-op House for African-American ministerial students attending Butler University; b) the establishment of a permanent scholarship fund in 1939 with money from a variety of sources; c) initiating the Star Supporter Scholarship Fund in 1948 through the leadership and promotion of the Convention's Christian Men's Fellowship and Ministers' Wives' Fellowship, and Ministers' Fellowship.

A task force of the laity and ministers was formed to promote the annual Star Supporter effort. Alfred Stone and Alfred Thomas, lay people from Cincinnati, Ohio; A. D. Gault, a lay leader from Mayslick, Kentucky; Samuel W. Hylton, Sr., a lay leader from Roanoke, Virginia; and Buford Hall, a lay leader from North Middletown, Kentucky, formed the central group. L. L. Dickerson from Columbus, Ohio became the principle minister giving the effort interpretation and promotional support.

Goals were set by the Christian Men's Fellowship and Ministers' Wives' Fellowship. A major event at each assembly of the National Convention was the recognition of donors and the Christian Men's Fellowship group, which had contributed the most money. The Convention then appointed a committee of five to work with the Department of Ministry in the United Christian Missionary Society in the making of scholarship grants.

## CHAPTER SIX

# THE CONVENTION DEVELOPS A SOCIAL CONSCIENCE (1930-1950)

Where is the Jim Crow section

On this merry-go-round,

Mister, cause I want to ride?

Down South where I come from

White and colored

Can't sit side by side.

Down South on the train

There's a Jim Crow car.

the bus we're put in the back-

But there ain't no back

To a merry-go-round!

Where's the horse

For a kid that's black?

—*Langston Hughes, 1942*

"The quota system as used by Butler University in the early thirties limited the number of Negro recruits for Christian leadership. It placed another obstacle which Negro college students had to overcome by establishing survival techniques in order to remain."

—*Emmett J. Dickson, former executive secretary of NCMC, 1980*

In 1930 the worst economic depression in the history was ravaging the nation. The NEW YORK TIMES announced (June 7) that the "n" in "Negro" would henceforth be capitalized, while former stock brokers and bankers joined unemployed laborers in soup lines.

Some of the tension spilled over into the Christian Church (Disciples of Christ), where Home Missions Work struggled to keep enough dollars on hand to operate, and interpersonal relations among staff and race relations were tested daily. Rosa Brown Bracy, the aggressive and effective Black staff woman who had served so well since 1914 offered her resignation during the February 12, 1930 meeting of the Joint Executive Committee. Following an executive session of the committee, it was accepted to become effective no later than June 30, 1930.[1] Reportedly, tense inter-staff relationships between Rosa Bracy and her Anglo-American peers was the rational for her resignation. Mrs. A. L. Martin of Chicago, who was the President of the National Christian Missionary Convention Women was asked to head a search committee to find Bracy's successor. Later, during the April 23, 1930 Joint Executive Committee meeting, it was "learned that the services of Rosa Brown Bracy as secretary, are available for that period of time between July 1, 1930 and the National Convention, August 25-31".[2]

The committee voted to continue her employment until the Convention. During the Convention, however, it was decided to maintain Mrs. Bracy and she was given the task of raising funds while working with the missionary groups.

During the Joint Executive Committee meeting on February 12, an historic signal was given to the church through a resolution. It had to do with the Joint Executive Committee's increased social consciousness of the many indignities suffered by African-American Disciples of Christ when they attempted to attend meetings together with Anglo-Americans. The resolution stated:

> "To avoid unnecessary embarrassment as respects the Pentecostal celebration in Washington, D. C.—Be it resolved that the representatives of the U C M S, holding membership on the Executive Committee, be asked to submit to the next Joint Executive Committee, complete information as to the registration, entertainment and freedom of access and participation by Negroes attending in Convention Hall or other places utilized for convention purposes at the Pentecostal celebration in 1930."[3]

Some responsible church leaders took the action seriously and Blacks attended the Pentecostal affair without incident.

## THE PLIGHT OF ANGLO-AMERICAN COLLEAGUES

During these early years, the Anglo-American counterparts of National Christian Missionary Convention leaders did not escape the negative impact of racism.  Bertha Mason Fuller recalled an incident involving a field visit to a small town in Texas by her father, Jacob Cason Mason Superintendent of Missions for Texas and J. B. Lehman of Southern Christian Institution Edwards, Mississippi.

Soon after they registered in the little hotel, it was quickly circulated around town that they had come to preach at the Negro Convention. Lehman suggested they eat in their room and not go outside to a restaurant for fear of stirring up trouble. But Mason replied "Brother Lehman, I am not doing anything I ought not do. I have fought to my own hurt (he was a veteran of the Civil War, blind in one eye and with other physical injuries) in the defense of the flag of my country and of the Union. I need a shave and I am going to a barber shop and get it, then have supper at the best restaurant in town. Will you go with me?".

The men went to the barbershop, where, to their surprise they were treated with suspicion at first but courtesy later.  They were accosted by some ruffians as they proceeded down the street to the restaurant, but ignored them and went into the restaurant and ate. They went to the Convention and stayed in town three days without further incident.[4]

## USE OF `THE CHRISTIAN PLEA'

African-Americans on the Joint Committee which administered program services to National Convention congregations attempted to secure control of a publication which would reflect the concerns and aspirations of Black Disciples. They had never thought that possible with THE GOSPEL PLEA. It was lodged on the campus of Southern Christian Institute in Edwards, Mississippi and under the predominant influence of J. B. Lehman.

After many meetings and Convention business sessions, action was taken for the National Convention to employ an editor who would print and circulate a paper called THE CHRISTIAN PLEA. Particular attention was given to the African-American perspective. This paper became a major vehicle for sharing activities and highlighting of experiences within the predominantly Black congregations and state organizations. Just prior to World War II and following, THE CHRISTIAN PLEA helped to reflect the new social consciousness abroad in the land.

Subscription support was weak, but the Joint Committee of the UCMS and National Convention were committed to underwriting the journal and Christian Board of Publication did the printing. Vance Smith of Danville, Kentucky did well as its first editor. Prince A. Gray of Kansas City, Missouri; Warren Brown, New York; C. H. Dickerson, Lexington, Kentucky; Merle R. Eppse, Nashville, Tennessee; and L. L. Dickerson of Columbus, Ohio followed in editorship. William K. Fox of St. Louis, Missouri closed out its life in 1959.

## DETERIORATING SOCIAL CLIMATE AND CHURCH RESPONSE

The decade of the thirties was not only plagued with the ravages of an economic depression and heroic efforts by President Franklin Delano Roosevelt to offset the total social as well economic devastation. It was the worst of times in every respect for African-Americans. Lynchings and the miscarriage of justice in the courts were frequent in the South. Blacks were usually the last hired and the first fired.

A mixture of factors within the Christian Church (Disciples of Christ) between the early 1930's and the mid 1940's were intertwined in a manner which made the church relevant to the troubled times. The response was low-key, church-centered and of good quality.

The operation of the National Convention as an ecclesiastical institution, provided invaluable training and experience for Black Disciples of Christ. It prepared them to function effectively within both the secular and religious communities. For example, the election of officers in a National Convention was usually a major Convention event. Possibly the most unusual as well as tragic election activity occurred during the 1936 Tulsa, Oklahoma, session when J. N. Ervin was eventually elected by a unanimous vote. The incumbent president, B. C. Calvert of Mississippi was so affected that he lost his sanity while delivering the closing sermon. A few hours later he died in a local infirmary from a stroke.

The only reward for securing the office of President of the Convention was the honor and respect. But that was a much sought after reward by the church leaders of that day. The Convention presidency gave visibility to Black Disciples of Christ and provided leadership experience for all associated.

## REACHING OUT TO YOUTH

In addition to editing THE CHRISTIAN PLEA, Vance Smith was responsible for religious education and youth work. Through his stimulation and nurture, a field visitation, institute and conference program was developed. They were sponsored by existing state organizations, mission schools and clusters of congregations. In Texas, the Piedmont (North Carolina, Virginia and West Virginia), and Kentucky, encouragement and training was given to leaders that had interest in youth.

The employment of Robert Hayes Peoples by the United Christian Missionary Society in 1935 as National Secretary of Negro Evangelism and Religious Education, marked an acceleration and improved coordination of concern for the training and nurture of young people and their leaders. He also brought into the Disciples of Christ church a ministerial leader with an innate ability to organize, strategize, and stimulate others to be more effective church persons.

His catalyzing presence was usually evident in the programing of the annual meeting of the National Christian Missionary Convention. This was especially true in regard to young people. Youth became involved in the music, leadership of worship for plenary sessions, special presentations, and had planned Christian Youth Fellowship training sessions. Key leaders of youth were mobilized to conduct these activities.

Helen E. Henry typified the interest and response from the states. In 1939 she heralded herself as "Texas Youth's Friend." Referring to the Texas Christian Missionary Convention, she reported, "For the first time in the history of the work, we have decided that some attention must be given to our young people, so we have added to our list a Director of Young People... We were happy over the beginning of the youth movement connected with our national convention...and desire to see a National Director of Youth on the field in very near future."[5]

In Mississippi where the first youth conference was held at Southern Christian Institute, Edwards, Mississippi in 1928, interest had dwindled by 1931. According to Jason Cowan, dean at S C I in 1939, national field workers R. H. Peoples, Vance Smith, and Carnella Jamison held "an experimental conference" for youth at S C I from March 27 to April 2, 1939. The "experiment" provided the push necessary to revive an interest in continuing the event.

## THE CONTRIBUTION OF WOMEN

African-American women among the Disciples of Christ had usually led the way in Christian missions as well as in religious education. In 1935, in addition to R. H. Peoples, the U C M S secured Carnella Jamison from Birmingham, Alabama to resource missionary groups and activities among National Convention women.

Jamison brought system and renewed dedication among the various mission groups. During the annual Conventions, the missionary organizations joined with the youth and men in sponsoring programs, which emphasized Christian mission and raised social consciousness.

Under the stimulus of Carnella Jamison in 1940 and the support of Willard Wickizer who was the Executive Secretary for the Church Development and Evangelism Program, Black women's mission groups were key in hosting the first National Interracial Field Visitation. The event brought encouragement to leadership in both races, and stimulated some of the White staff in states and areas to seriously consider the importance of servicing all congregations in their jurisdiction, without regard to race or color.

## WORLD WAR II

The advent of World War II made the development of a social consciousness on the part of the National Christian Missionary Convention a corporate "must." During these years Foster and Alberta Craggett of Cleveland, Ohio were key among several volunteers like Charles Sherman, Paul Sims, Edna Brown, Thomas Griffin, and Ozark Range, Sr. who provided strategic services and programs for youth during the National Convention Annual Sessions.

Young African-Americans and Anglo-Americans were being inducted into the armed forces and were dying together on far-flung battlefields. In 1940 the annual meeting of the National Convention in Little Rock, Arkansas, dealt with the racial issue head-on. Workshops were confronted with the following questions:

1.   What is the procedure for questioning the evil of race hatred?

2.  What can the Negro do to eliminate this evil?

3.  What can White people do to eliminate race hatred and discrimination?

## CHICAGO DISCIPLES DIVINITY HOUSE

Dr. Merle R. Eppse, Professor of History in Nashville's, Tennessee State College, succeeded C. H. Dickerson as editor of The CHRISTIAN PLEA in 1940. His initial use of the Convention paper was to expose the practices of racial discrimination in the entrance procedures at Disciples of Christ-related colleges and seminaries.

Emmett J. Dickson and R. H. Peoples made unsuccessful attempts to secure Chicago Disciples House fellowships. All evidence pointed toward racism. Eventually an agreement was reached between the National Convention and the Disciples Divinity House Dean Edward Scribner Ames, that if any Black Disciple was found who met both Divinity School and House criteria, that person would be accepted for a Disciples House fellowship.

Following declaration for ministry, William K. Fox, a history major under Dr. Eppse was accepted by the University of Chicago and granted a Divinity School tuition scholarship. But the Disciples house refused to grant Mr. Fox a fellowship, which provided residence and a monthly stipend. Eppse kept the matter before Black Disciples of Christ through THE CHRISTIAN PLEA. African-Americans supported Fox's quest for a Divinity House Fellowship. E. C. and Rosa Page Welch provided Fox with housing during his first quarter's matriculation in the University's Divinity School.[6]

In April of l941 Fox was awarded the scholarship through a personal telephone call from Dean E. S. Ames. He became the first Black Disciples of Christ to receive a House Fellowship. He remained to complete and receive his Bachelor of Divinity Degree.[7]

## ON THE FIELD

National church staff had always provided the majority of field services and help to predominantly Black Disciples of Christ congregations. However, in 1942 when the Joint Executive Committee administration of work among National Convention churches concept was dropped and a vehicle known as the Inter-Agency Council adopted, an effort was initiated to encourage the state and area employed church staff to include African-American churches and church structures in their field services. The following policy was proposed and circulated among the states and areas:

It is the opinion of this committee, that the question of brotherhood service to certain National groups, especially to Negro churches in the Southern States, needs clarification as to thoughts, privileges, and responsibilities of missionary service and guidance, and it therefore recommends that those states in which the state missionary societies have the disposition to do so, such state societies be requested to approach Negro conventions, Negro churches or other groups of Negro Disciples of Christ to offer counsel, guidance and missionary service extended to all other churches or groups by the state society.[8]

Improved race relations became a high priority for both the National Christian Missionary Convention and the United Christian Missionary Society. December 3-4, 1944, at the urging of the Inter-Agency Council, a Conference on Relationships Between the NCMC and the UCMS was held in Indianapolis, Indiana. Principles for self-development and cooperation were set forth during the conference, which became background for later steps taken toward full partnership in mission.

Black staff field experiences documented racism. Thomas J. Griffin, who in 1945 became the first African-American professional staff employed in the Department of Social Welfare of the United Christian Missionary Society, made an interesting report on his involvement in an incident which appeared to have racial overtones. His field schedule called for him to go to Wilson, North Carolina, as a leader in an all-Anglo-American youth conference. Instead as he left Washington, D. C., en route to Wilson, he received a telegram from Indianapolis, Indiana saying not to go to Wilson but instead report to Charles H. Webb, minister of Cleveland Avenue Christian Church in Winston-Salem, N. C.

No one told Griffin why he should make the change in destinations. A few weeks later while in Indianapolis, a young man who had been a faculty member at the conference, approached Griffin and made himself known. He said that "he wanted so very badly to see Griffin there, but the director felt the time wasn't right since they never had a Negro participate in one of their conferences..." [9]

Later when the Convention employed Lorenzo Evans as director of Christian education in 1947, the involvement of children and youth was strengthened. A National Christian Education Planning Council was developed which advanced ideas about laboratory training schools for children and youth workers.

In addition, to dramatize the need to encourage youth in free expression and the nurturing of speech skills, a National Youth Oratorical Contest was organized as an annual feature of the National Convention. The following were the objectives for the contest:

* To develop expression of original thought and work;

* To encourage youth in the local church to become aware of their responsibilities as Christians and dedicate themselves to the task;

* To encourage and promote Christian training;

* To help youth realize that formal training is a must if they are to cope favorably with the world in which they find themselves; and

* To help youth become better acquainted with contemporary problems and issues.

The oratorical contest proved to be a stellar event at the National Convention. Monetary awards and plaques were given to the first three winners and certificates were given to all participants.

## THE YOUTH CONFERENCE AND SOCIAL CONSCIOUSNESS

The Youth Conference experience was supposed to spread to the congregation and into daily living. Happenings for young people at the annual meeting of the National Christian Missionary Convention during those years was essentially an extended Youth Conference experience. Equally important, the United Christian Missionary Society, through its Youth Services Program and the directorship of George Oliver Taylor, made intentional effort to use the Youth Conference setting to foster racial understanding.

During the early 1940's it was established UCMS policy to deploy a "missionary" as a special Conference leader. The "missionary" Conference leader was sometimes African-American in a traditionally all-Anglo-American Youth Conference, or Anglo-American in a traditionally all-African-American Youth Conference. The "missionary" brought the vesper messages, taught a Conference course, and shared special leadership gifts. Eventually these "missionary" leaders were sometimes the Conference Dean.

One of these Conference "missionary leaders" who developed into a world renowned figure as an "Ambassador of Goodwill" was Rosa Page Welch, a product of Southern Christian Institute and resident of Chicago, Illinois. During the Centennial Celebration of the International Convention in Cincinnati, Ohio, October 25-30, 1949, Rosa Page became the first African-American Disciple chosen by the Program Committee to lead Convention singing.

## INFUSION OF SELECT CONVENTION SESSION SPEAKERS

Persons chosen by the Program Committees during this period of social consciousness raising included African-American Disciples of Christ leaders and others who could bring a challenging and substantive message. During the Twenty-sixth Annual Convention held in Nashville, Tennessee, August 17-23, 1942, George E. Haynes, Race Relation's Executive for the Federal Council of Churches (now National Council of Churches of Christ in the United States), addressed the plenary session on "The Church and War Services." Then Haynes held seminar sessions and discussions with ministers and church board members. He also resourced discussions in the social education and missionary education conferences on "interracial relations in our communities in relation to the war situation."

Through James Crain, Director of the Social Welfare Department of the UCMS, the National Convention received updating presentations on social, economic and justice issues during seminar sessions. Discussion was usually moderated by a National Convention African-American leader. Eventually a Convention Social Action Commission was formed (1952) and Lewis A. Deer became the first UCMS Social Welfare Department staff provided to resource its research and activity.

## CHAPTER SEVEN

# MOVEMENT TOWARD PARTNERSHIP PHASE I: THE CONVENTION EMPLOYS STAFF AND PROVIDES SERVICES (1935-1959)

That they all may be one—that is the goal of the Disciples. A movement among the churches and in the church interracial and international to recreate the spirit of tolerance, forbearance and love exemplified in the early church among all Christians everywhere, regardless of color or race.
—*"Two Races in One Fellowship" by R. L. Jordan, 1944*

A truly catholic, evangelical, and reformed church is a "big bubbly stew," where all parts of the church are mixed, and recognized, and respected as having a legitimate right to be where they are and to contribute together to the purpose of the church.
—*"Another View of What is Needed," by Anne E. Dickerson, THE UNTOLD STORY, 1976*

From the very beginning in 1917 the fathers and mothers of the National Christian Missionary Convention pressed for cooperation with national church organizations in carrying out the work. Striving to be cooperative and laboring valiantly to maintain a high level of human dignity, Convention founders worked with many Anglo-Americans who were paternalistic.

Soon after the Great Depression and the employment of R. H. Peoples as the National Field Secretary in 1936, NCMC leadership gradually began to support the concepts of self-endowed with divine blessings and partnership with all others engaged in Christian mission.

Half of Peoples' time was spent under the administration of the Department of Church Development and Evangelism. He had the responsibility for planning and directing the Program of Evangelism and Church Maintenance, which once had been the sole responsibility of J. B. Lehman.

The other half of R. H. Peoples' task was within the Department of Religious Education. He was solely responsible for the religious education emphasis for African-American congregations a responsibility previously shared by Deetsey Blackburn and Patrick H. Moss.

Peoples was a tireless worker on the field. As previously noted, he gave meticulous time to the development of youth meetings and conferences, and later Chi-Rho camps. He nurtured state conventions like a "devoted shepherd of the flock". One example is his service to the South Carolina Christian Missionary Convention, which had long drawn heavily upon guidance from the national office.

During the sixty-eighth annual session of that Convention held October 4-8, 1939, in Holly Hill, South Carolina. Peoples sent an "open letter" to the South Carolina churches as background for the response he wanted to receive from them when he visited the convention. The letter began:

> "Dear Friends: The greatest adventure ever launched by any of our state conventions has been started in your state. It is not only a great adventure, but it is a new one and one we feel will help solve the problem of the rural church. As you look at the picture of this beautiful building that has been proposed for your consideration, just remember that only one thing will make this dream come true, and that is OUR MOTTO: EVERY MEMBER AND FRIEND BUY A BRICK FOR THE NEW CHURCH..."

Secretary Peoples then specified how much money was needed to buy one brick on up to 5,000 bricks and how every elder, deacon, state officer, member of a local church and family could raise the money. People were trying to demonstrate that people could build a beautiful, functional church building in the rural areas. The project illustrates the intensity and dedication, which he applied to his field responsibilities.1 But, he was only one Black staff person.

Soon after Peoples' employment in 1936, Carnella Jamison was secured to give two-thirds of a year to direct a program of organizing mission groups and promoting mission education under the administration of the UCMS Department of Missionary Organization-Education. In July 1942 this position became full-time. Fieldwork, once done with minimum financial support by Sarah Lue Bostick and Rosa Brown Bracey, was now being given a priority equal to the other aspects of the church at work.

In 1943 at the height of World War II, it was the resignation of R. H. Peoples and his departing report, which highlighted the first milestone toward partnership in the mission. During the twenty-sixth annual National Christian Missionary Convention in Columbus, Ohio, Peoples devoted his final report to sketching a history of the development of Christian Church (Disciples of Christ) services to predominantly Black congregations with particular references to the relationships of the NCMC.

National Field Secretary Peoples ended his summary with the following conclusion:

> "It is my judgment, after nearly eight years of service as field worker for the Departments of Church Development and Evangelism and Religious Education that the Disciples' program of work among  Negro churches and educational institutions should be as follows:

1. The work of the departments within the United Christian Missionary Society should be planned jointly by all the departments within the Society that have programs of work among Negroes.

2. That the administration of this work might be assigned to one of the departments within the UCMS. The UCMS should add Negro members to the board of trustees.

3. That other national brotherhood agencies with programs of work among Negroes should be invited to cooperate both in the planning and administering of this program.

4. That the United Christian Missionary Society and other cooperating boards (such as the Pension Fund, Church Extension, Higher Education and Christian Board of Publication) employ a staff adequate to help plan and administer this program. That these workers be given the same status as other national workers in the cooperating boards.

5. That the following list of workers should be considered as the minimum:

a.    A general worker to handle general administration and work with ministers and church boards.

b.    A women's worker to develop the women of the Negro brotherhood.

c.    A young people's worker to work with Sunday schools and Christian Youth Fellowship groups.

d.    A children's worker to develop adequate program for children.

e.    An evangelist to develop a broad evangelistic program.

f.    A promotional worker who would direct the promotion of all phases of the     work and edit THE CHRISTIAN PLEA.

I have given these recommendations because I hope they will at least point the direction that the Convention will take as we seek to develop the Negro churches as an integral part of the total brotherhood..."[1]

## THE RESPONSE TO PEOPLES' REPORT

The vision for future operations of the National Christian Missionary Convention and the United Christian Missionary Society which climaxed R. H. Peoples' final report was placed in formalized recommendations and sent to the UCMS from the Convention. They, indeed, were destined to mold the direction of National Convention/ UCMS relationships for the remainder of the century.

A long-range program committee was appointed out of the Columbus Convention and Sere S. "S.S." Myers of Kansas City, Missouri was appointed chairman. The Committee went to work immediately. Myers, a classmate of Peoples and long time ministerial associate, was chairman of the steering committee, which had established the Tri-State Missionary Board for Kansas, Missouri and Oklahoma in 1939. This Board consisted of the Anglo-American secretaries from the state societies and three members from each of the African-American state conventions in those states. They had employed R. Wesley Watson of Kansas City, Missouri as their state evangelist.

Myers drew heavily upon this experience as he gave leadership to the National Convention's Long Range Planning Committee. He was working as a bi-vocational pastor in Kansas City, and dividing his time between Kansas City, Missouri, Indianapolis, Indiana and field visitations. Myers promoted the idea of the National Convention employing its own staff, establishing its own headquarter's, and providing full consultation services and nurture to congregations affiliated with the Convention.

When the Convention met in Lexington, Kentucky for its twenty-seventh session, Chairman Myers presented the following report:

Mr. President and delegates, we, your Committee on Long Range Planning wish to submit the following report. During the year we have had several meetings at which we reviewed the present status of our brotherhood; our future needs, our relationship with the United Christian Missionary Society, and ways and means by which we can preserve this relationship and at the same time have a larger part in determining policies and directing the work now being done by the United Christian Missionary Society and other brotherhood agencies among Negroes.

We have held conferences with Dr. Robert H. Hopkins, President of the UCMS, Mr. W. M. Wickizer, Secretary of the Department of Home Missions, Mr. George O. Taylor, and Mr. Virgil E. Havens. As a result of these conferences, we submit the following report:

1. That the National Board of this Convention take over such functions of the Negro Work now being done by the UCMS and other brotherhood agencies as they may be agreed upon by the National Board, UCMS and such Aother agencies@. That the Board employ its own staff and establish its own headquarters office, location to be determined by the National Board. That the Staff direct the programs of Evangelism, Religious Education, Church Development, Pension Fund, Benevolence, Scholarships, Church Extension, Higher Education, Financial Resources, Enlistment of full-time workers and THE CHRISTIAN PLEA.

2. That the Constitution be amended to allow representation from the UCMS and such other brotherhood agencies cooperating, membership on the National Board.

COMMITTEE: S. S. Myers, Chairman, R. H. Peoples, Dr. J. E. Walker, W. H. Taylor, L. L. Dickerson, Cleo Blackburn, C. L. Parks, Carnella Jamison, Elizabeth Herod. (p. 4 of 1944 NCMC minutes)[2]

## THE RESPONSE OF LEXINGTON CONVENTION REPRESENTATIVES

The 1944 Convention was possibly the most explosive in the largely passive existence of the organization. W. H. Taylor of Baltimore, Maryland, had been elected president during the 1942 session in Kansas City, Missouri. During his administration he had successfully promoted the idea that God had blessed African-American people and that it was their Christian duty to share some of these blessings for the advancement of the Christian endeavor. Taylor was a traditionalist in theology and a fervent advocate of the simplistic presentation of Disciples of Christ doctrine.

The combination of Taylor's emphasis upon Black Disciples of Christ using their own resources to help themselves plus his insistence upon purity in practice and belief in the Disciples doctrine, became a potent reactionary force confronting the Convention leaders who were pressing for a new stance in relationships with the United Christian Missionary Society and other church agencies. The whole matter came to a head during the discussion on the long range planning report and eventually in the election of the new Convention president.

The Meyer's Long Range Commission had negotiated a plan, which called for the National Convention to:

1. Employ its own staff;

2. Establish its own headquarter's;

3. Edit and print its own newspaper;

4. Provide all of the agency services lodged in the various national agencies;

5. Revise the Convention constitution to provide for board memberships on the Convention's National Board for all agencies supporting the new arrangement; and to,

6. Receive a share of financial support from each of the national agencies for which, in fact, national Black staff would be representing in the Convention churches.

Opposition to the plan rested mainly on the argument that Blacks would not, in fact, be in control of the program. James Blair maintains that the real issue of this Convention was the establishment of a National Convention office in Indianapolis, Indiana, at the Missions Building. The opposition felt that the office in the Missions Building would be dominated and controlled by the Anglo-American people. Those "for" the Indianapolis office felt that Indianapolis was centrally located and to establish the office some place else would look like division and give the National Convention a "Jim Crow" brand.

The Commission maintained that the plan would achieve the following objectives:

1.  To serve as an instrument to integrate the Negro membership into the organized life of the brotherhood and to give them a sense of belonging to the whole,

2.  To provide an adequate program to meet the needs of the church in the following areas—(a) evangelism, (b) education, (c) missions, (d) stewardship, (e) pension and relief, (f) church extension, (g) higher education, (h) Christian literature, and (i) benevolence;

3.  To give better service and more cultivation to the local churches in order that they may be challenged to greater participation in kingdom building; and

4.  To provide greater opportunity for Negro leadership to participate in planning and directing the program of Negro churches.

Prior to the final consideration of the Commission report, C. L. Parks, had been employed to assume that part of R. H. Peoples' job which dealt with church development and evangelism. During the presentation he challenged remarks W. H. Taylor had made in his president's message which dealt with doctrinal matters and implied future Convention officers should be proven "true Disciples" before they were elected. Officially, Parks' remarks were not recognized by the body.

However, when the Commission report came up for a final vote, intense discussion ensued on the Convention floor. The loyalists to W. H. Taylor and some Anglo-American opportunists from the independent Church of Christ movement who were present, seized the moment of heated debate to inject the notion of "open membership." Some held that no true Disciple of Christ would want to associate with those people in the Missions Building who advocated "open membership" (i. e. the acceptance of people from other denominations as members who had not been baptized by immersion). This became their "rallying cry" for others to join their ranks.

The supporters of the Long Range Commission plan won the vote. The debate went on into the election of officers for the new Convention year. The committee brought in the name of S. S. Meyers, of Kansas City, Missouri. The Independents nominated W. H. Taylor when the house opened for nominations from the floor. R. H. Davis of Chicago, Illinois, received thirty-eight votes, W. H. Taylor fifty-one votes and S. S. Myers received 191 votes. W. H. Taylor walked out of the Convention with a group of ministers who were in sympathy with racial independence. Others who did not understand the way the campaign had been waged left because they felt that such methods were undemocratic and unchristian.

Many in this group were ministers who answered the call of Taylor to form a "National Christian Preaching Convention." It held annual meetings for a time, received some support from the independent Church of Christ movement, and published a paper edited by W. H. Taylor   called THE CHRISTIAN INFORMER. The paper's masthead carried the slogan "a monthly publication Devoted to the Restoration of Primitive Christianity, its Doctrine, its Ordinances and its Fruits".

By 1950 most ministers who left with Taylor returned to the main Disciples body. They recognized commonality in the quest of Restoration goals and Christian democracy. James Blair maintains that "the National Convention in 1944 became a group working for the integration of the African-American and Anglo-American work but bitterly opposed to absorption into the larger body where their voices advocating meeting the needs of African-American people would be weakened".[3]

S. S. Myers was elected president of the Convention for two terms and thus helped guide the implementation of the new plan of operation during its formative years. The first order of business was the development of a staff, which was competent in carrying out the ambitious vision. The comparable concern was the motivation of the congregations to raise their level of giving to the Convention, which was now charged with providing a full range of program services.

## DEVELOPING A STAFF

The initial search went out for what R. H. Peoples had termed "general worker to handle general administration and work with the ministers and church boards." C. L. Parks who had been a Flanner House staff person in Indianapolis, Indiana, was employed in 1944 to do part of what National Negro Secretary Peoples had been doing. He directed institutes for ministers and related to evangelistic events sponsored by congregations and the organized African-American state and regional conventions.

In the late 1920's, while serving a problem plagued Grove Street Christian Church in Houston, Texas, S. S. Myers first met Emmett J. Dickson of Crockett, Texas and formed what he calls "a life-long friendship." The two worked together to assist Grove Street Church.

Memories of this association came back to Myers as the Convention search committee worked to find qualified candidates for the general administrative staff position. Dickson, a Jarvis College faculty member in 1945, was eventually chosen to become the first (and only) Executive Secretary of the National Christian Missionary Convention.

Carnella Jamison was the successor to Rosa Brown Bracey. She had been working in the field among the women as national secretary of missionary organizations while completing her studies at Chicago Theological Seminary. In the fall of 1943 she returned to Indianapolis to give full-time service.

Lorenzo Evans of Atlanta, Georgia, had been serving as Program Secretary of the Butler Street YMCA. He came to the staff in 1946 as the Director of Christian Education. C. L. Parks eventually accepted a challenge from the Churches of Christ, Disciples of Christ in the Goldsboro-Raleigh District to cooperate with the United Christian Missionary Society in up grading their Minister's Institute Program. In 1949 Charles H. Webb of Winston-Salem, North Carolina, made his first report to the annual meeting of the Convention as the new Director of Church Development and Evangelism.

## LEADERSHIP TRAINING AND DEVELOPMENT

The first five years in the operation of the new self-development emphasis of the National Convention staff was spent mainly on leader training and development. Against the background of post-war America, the Christian Church (Disciples of Christ) launched a "Crusade for a Christian World" (1948-51). This church-wide emphasis gave the new Convention staff impetus and a variety of resources to push leader training and development.

The National Convention had assumed specific goals which included: (a) 24,000 new members (12,000 by baptism and 12,000 by transfer); (b) twenty new congregations; (c) one hundred recruits to the ministry; ten new pastoral unities organized involving at least thirty rural congregations; plus realization of financial goals for mission giving and Week of Compassion. These activities and more were a part of the Disciples of Christ response to rebuilding the war-torn world.

In addition, as National Director of Christian Education Evans urged Convention-affiliated congregations to emphasize church school enlargement, trained leaders, Christian family life, and missionary education. In 1945 C. L. Parks directed five institutes for ministers from February through April 6 at Jarvis College, Hawkins, Texas, for ministers in Oklahoma and Arkansas; in Kansas City for ministers in Missouri, Kansas and Iowa; in Martinsville, Virginia, for ministers of the Tri-State and Piedmont areas; in Goldsboro, North Carolina, for ministers in Western and North Carolina; and at Southern Christian Institute, Edwards, Mississippi, for ministers of Mississippi, west Tennessee, and Alabama. This vigorous effort was continued by his successor, Charles H. Webb, Sr.

During the Christmas holidays of 1947-48 Parks led a series of Visitation Evangelism Clinics for ministers in seven strategically located centers. Leadership training, beginning with the minister, was the priority.

By 1947 Lorenzo J. Evans had recruited a significant number of qualified volunteers to sponsor the first National Conference on Christian Education of the National Christian Missionary Convention during the Cincinnati, Ohio, annual meeting. There was something for every church leader and every organization in the congregation. Bessie E. Chandler of St. Louis, Missouri, former staff employee of Christian Woman's Board of Missions, became a key volunteer director and coordinator of this religious education thrust.

Heretofore, the "Observation Bible School" was the principle model used by religious educators to communicate methods and concepts. But it was usually limited to biblical materials and sometimes narrow in its application of principles to contemporary life and work. The Conference idea, running as an integral part of the Convention meeting, provided a setting for Christian education activity to be experienced by all persons attending the convention.

The conference concept involved two hours a day for classes with the first hour being lecture and discussion and the second hour used for organization and promotional concerns.

The Director of Christian Education sponsored a Fall Planning Conference at Thanksgiving time for state, area and selected congregational workers to review, evaluate and project programs for the Convention. Convention officers and age-level fellowship presidents were expected to attend and do serious planning for the next National Convention as well as state and area events.

The women's mission groups, for example, selected a "national project" for each year. Then the groups were encouraged to bring "gifts" to the next Convention for that project. On "Women's Night" the various mission groups would bring their "gifts" forward as an act of worship.

## CHRISTIAN STEWARDSHIP

A critical part of the new Convention stance was the giving of financial support by the congregations. The young, inexperienced staff was being pressed by the editors of THE CHRISTIAN PLEA and others to make reports, which justified the new financial obligations of the congregations.

The executive secretary was expected to not only maintain the financial commitments already made from the cooperating agencies, but to cultivate the Convention congregations to give. Goals were set for congregations, state, and area conventions. Financial reports often appeared in THE CHRISTIAN PLEA. The Executive Secretary sent many notes like the following:

Elder L. L. Dickerson
Columbus, Ohio

"Dear Brother Dickerson:

The Executive Committee of the National Christian Missionary Convention has authorized me to appoint you to promote the financial cause of the National Convention in the states of Ohio and Kentucky. I am sending you the goals of each church in Ohio and Kentucky. You will note that the goal for Ohio is $1,576.00 and for Kentucky, $1,974.00... I shall be glad to help you in this big effort."

Sincerely,
*Emmett J. Dickson (June 1948)*

Besides sharing support staff for the servicing of conventions and other gatherings of African-American Disciples of Christ, during the first five years of the new operational plan the cooperating agencies contributed about half of the operating budget. The following table reflects the nature of budget support.

## TABLE 4

### NCMC FINANCIAL SUPPORT FOR 1949, 1953 &1955

| SOURCE OF INCOME | 1949 | 1953 | 1956 |
|---|---|---|---|
| United Christian Missionary Society | 12000 | 12999 | 14500 |
| National Benevolent Association | 600 | 750 | 750 |
| Pension Fund | 650 | 600 | 600 |
| Board of Church Extension | --- | 600 | 1500 |
| Board of Higher Education | 750 | 300 | --- |
| Christian Board of Publication | 2000 | 3000 | --- |
| Crusade for a Christian World Funds | 2500 | 1000 | --- |
| National Christian Missionary Convention | 8321 | 12593 | 15137 |
| NCMC Taylor Estate (Greenwood Cemetery) | --- | 2800 | 4000 |

*Source: J. E. Walker, NCMC Treasurer's Reports, 1949

[Note: NCMC accepted a $50,000 goal in the $14 million program of "Crusade for a Christian World" (1947-50). They had given $13,199.18 by May 5,1949.]

Contributions from predominantly Black congregations came in slowly. In 1948 a significant legal transaction occurred in Nashville, Tennessee. A decree of the Chancier Court gave the Preston Taylor estate to the National Christian Missionary Convention. Thus, as planned by the courageous prophet and benefactor, Preston Taylor, an important permanent resource was provided the infant Christian body struggling valiantly to become a mature and equal partner in the mission.

## CONVENTION LAITY TACKLE THE PREPARED MINISTRY CHALLENGE

Under the stimulus of a cadre of creative lay people in 1949, the entire convention structure was challenged to support the recruitment, training and placement of young ministers. Alfred Thomas and Alfred C. Stone of Cincinnati, Ohio; Norman S. Ellington of St. Louis, Missouri; Buford Hall of North Middletown, Kentucky; A. D. Gault, Mayslick, Kentucky, with support from ministers Dickerson of Columbus, Ohio, and Charles Webb, Sr, of the Convention staff, formed a combine of leaders which designed and promoted the "Star Supporter Fund".

Every lay member and minister was challenged to give at least ten dollars per year toward the formal preparation of ministers. CMF groups in the congregations were asked to spearhead the effort and bring the money to the annual session of the convention. At that point the CMF sponsored a dinner, had one of the "Star Supporter" recipients of a scholarship speak, and awarded a traveling plaque to the CMF group reporting the most money. Promotion of the project was the key responsibility of the national CMF chairman.

By 1952 these lay people had become so intentional in their effort, that they considered the national CMF chairman a "one dollar a year convention staff person." The new Convention President, L. L. Dickerson, had been an enthusiastic backer. Alfred Thomas, who was president of the Convention CMF, came to the December 16-17, 1952 Board Meeting with a detailed report on the goals for the Christian Men's Fellowship which included: (a) securing a field worker to do evangelistic training, promotion and enlistment; (b) a library project for the Taylor Memorial Fellowship House; (c) the raising of special monies; and (d) a laity retreat. Unfortunately, Thomas died during the 1954 annual session in St. Louis, Missouri, before he was to make the first report to the main body on the progress of his pioneering work.

The Ministers Wives' Fellowship of the convention joined the effort in a similar fashion. A part of their activities during the annual session of the Convention was a "crowning of the Minister's Wives Queen" from the state or area where minister's wives reported the most money for ministerial scholarships. The ceremonies for announcing the amount of money raised by wives and the "crowning" was both a serious and gala affair witnessed by all Convention attendants.

The Star Supporter Fund soon joined the mission project promotion of the Christian Women's Fellowship as the only long-standing Christian stewardship effort to receive the whole-hearted support of a majority of National Convention congregations.

A major financial promotional meeting was held at the Mance Hotel in Cincinnati, Ohio on January 24, 1953. A cross-section of National Convention leaders assembled at the call of Lorenzo J. Evans and Emmett J. Dickson. Representatives from Unified Promotion [i. e. the "United Fund" aspect of the Christian Church (Disciples of Christ) at the time] were present. Plans were made to increase giving from the National Convention congregations.

In 1956 the National Board of Trustees appointed Alfred C. Stone of Cincinnati, Ohio, Director of Financial Promotion and an intensive effort was launched to deal seriously with the financial support of the Convention.

An attempt was made to divide the Convention into eight promotional areas with a director for each. A survey revealed eighty congregations as fairly consistent givers, with thirty-eight of them contributing ninety-five percent of the money from the churches. The thirty-eight were given intensive cultivation through team visitations and letters. During 1959, the year of the forty-third annual session in Dallas, Texas, August 17-23, the thirty-eight congregations reached their combined goal of $15,745.91. That was for only thirty-eight congregations out of the 546!

Increased efforts continued toward achieving the goal of racial integration within the church bureaucracy. A significant report on the merger of program services was to be presented to the 1959 annual Convention session in Dallas, Texas.

The effort to improve Christian stewardship was in fact a companion effort to the process for achieving integration goals. But this intent was never fully realized. As merger goals became realized, there remained a reluctance on the part of many congregations in the unorganized areas to go all out in giving financial support to the National Convention. While in the long established organized states and areas African-American congregations continued to give major financial support to their own substructures.

## CHAPTER EIGHT

# PHASE II: BUILDING TOWARD MERGER OF NCMC PROGRAM AND SERVICES (1952–1960)

> You can no more come from where you ain't been than do that which you don't know.
> —*Favorite Aunt Matilda quote by Cleo W. Blackburn (1909-1978), Black Disciples of Christ educator, sociologist, minister*

The first five years of employing and maintaining a staff to provide the full gamut of direct field services had provided an increasingly challenging experience for leadership at all levels.

Staff had come a long way from the dawning days of the twentieth century when the highest salary was fifty dollars per month and often expense money depended upon the size of the collection following a sermon or address. Workloads were heavy then and under the new program of operations they became even heavier.

## CHURCH DEVELOPMENT AND EVANGELISM

A vigorous and dedicated Restoration doctrinal preacher, L. L. Dickerson, who had been editor of THE CHRISTIAN PLEA and Convention Secretary, succeeded the smooth administrator and promoter, S. S. Myers, as president. Under the stimulus of Charles H. Webb, Sr., Director of Church Development and Evangelism, plans for establishing a new congregation in Mobile, Alabama were made, and interest in doing the same in Atlanta, Georgia expressed. Linkage was made with local White Disciples of Christ in Mobile and the state church society of Alabama, and the project became a reality.

Spurred by the prevailing need for prepared African-American pastors, the Taylor Memorial Fellowship House was launched. The Convention's age-level fellowships were caught up in giving the venture practical support. Resources from the church and individuals were mobilized to purchase a house near the Butler University campus in Indianapolis; make minimum renovations; install furnishings and equipment; recruit students; employ staff; and provide oversight and management by the Director of Church Development and Evangelism as well as the Executive Secretary. The promotion and maintenance of the project became an overwhelming responsibility.

In 1957 the Taylor House had some outstanding indebtedness and Webb was searching for a "consecrated born again Disciple" who would give "two $10,000 donations."[1]

While the Director for Church Development and Evangelism was trying to be "Dean" of a campus-related seminarian's house, there was no let up on the field. The attempts to bring about either a merger or the establishment of a new congregation in Jackson, Mississippi, is a good example.

In 1954, through the urging of First Christian Church in Jackson and key leaders in the two African-American congregations, Dr. Webb involved key executives and staff A. Dale Fiers, Willard Wickizer and Fred Michel in trying to guide Disciples of Christ in Jackson, Mississippi, toward merger or a new congregation. By 1957 the College Addition and Farish Street congregations in Jackson, Mississippi, had agreed on merger. National staff promised them assistance in securing adequate funds to buy a site and build a new church structure.

## CHRISTIAN EDUCATION

Within this same five-year period, Lorenzo J. Evans, Director of Christian Education, was also deeply involved. Besides initiating and administering a comprehensive religious education and leader training program, Mr. Evans had begun to call upon his program delivery system to do Christian stewardship education and financial promotion.

Evans initiated a program during the denomination's "Decade of Decision" (i.e. 1950-1960) that included: (a) children's work; (b) recruitment and training of church volunteers; (c) work with intermediates and their leaders; (d) senior and older young people's programs; (e) training of volunteers in "state work;" (f) developing meaningful relationships with church youth in college; (g) young adult and adult programs; (h) conferences and events for church school superintendents in educational administration; and (i) institutes on family life.

Probably the most impressive church-wide project sponsored under Dr. Evan's administration and the encouragement of George Oliver Taylor, the Executive Secretary for Christian Education, was the Kenneth Henry/Newton Fowler Christian Youth Fellowship Project. Approved by the National Convention Board of Trustees during the 1952 Annual Convention in Los Angeles, California, sufficient funds were given by congregations and individuals for these two young men to be delegates to the Third World Youth Conference in Travancore, India, in 1953. Upon their return, the interracial team made an impressive tour of the congregations throughout the nation sensitizing them—many for the first time—to their responsibilities as members of the universal Church.

Director Evans broadened his interests as well as the vision of the National Convention's board of trustees in 1957-58 when he sought and received their approval of a three-month's travel study. During that time he attended the fourteenth World Convention on Christian Education in Tokyo, Japan, August 6-13, 1958.

## MISSIONARY EDUCATION AND WOMEN'S GROUPS

Meanwhile, Anna Belle Jackson, Director of Missionary Education and Christian Women's Fellowship, was immersed in the work of women's groups. Her administrative load included planning and leading church worker's conferences and schools of mission in the various southern and mid-western states.

Workers conferences were events where the three Convention program directors acted as a team to guide the participants in understanding the relationships between district, state and national church work. This called for the cooperation and involvement of employed Anglo-American staff persons who were available at any or all levels. Representatives from each major program group in the congregation were invited to these events.

In 1957 after six and one-half years of service, Jackson was proud to observe:

"We have just completed a year where the ministry in our brotherhood has been the emphasis. Our CWF groups have been instrumental in securing funds for certain ministerial students to be applied to scholarships for the furtherance of their education. Programs have been geared to the Year of the Ministry and consecrated efforts have been made to get commitments from young men and women for full-time Christian service..."

Director Jackson was referring to help which had been given to seminarians like Gerald Cunningham and Donald Gibbs of St. Louis, Missouri, and James Brooks of Cincinnati, Ohio.

Progress in the work of the church through women's groups was marked with practicality through an adoption of service projects, which enabled every type of group—large or small—to share in an effort and be counted, important. Further, the women, along with the church schools, became the major means for mission education in congregations.

Equally important during the 1950's, or the Christian Church (Disciples of Christ)'s "Decade of Decision Campaign," were the signal contributions of Black women to Christendom as a whole. Their actions provided models for the women in Convention congregations to continue to be faithful in the work.

Most notable in this respect was Rosa Page Welch of Chicago, Illinois, who, in August, 1952, started an eight-month trip around the world as an "ambassador of goodwill." She was sponsored by the Presbyterian Board of Missions which initiated the project; the Disciples of Christ's United Christian Missionary Society; the Disciples Minister's Wives' Fellowship; the Department of United Church Women of the National Council of Churches; and the Women's American Baptist Foreign Mission Society.

Welch spent from two to six weeks on mission locations in Tokyo, Japan; the Philippines; the World Conference of Christian Youth in Travancore, India; the annual convention of Christian Churches in Jabalpur, India; Thailand; Pakistan; Beirut, Lebanon; French Cameroons; Belgian Congo (now Zaire); visiting the World Council of Churches in Geneva, Switzerland, and other European countries. Welch returned and traveled extensively among congregations and major events within all five sponsoring church groups. She gave testimony to her experiences at a plenary session during the International Convention of the Disciples of Christ on July 7, 1953, at Portland, Oregon.

On June 19-23, 1957, the first quadrennial assembly of the International Christian Women's Fellowship of the Disciples of Christ was sponsored on the Purdue University campus, Lafayette, Indiana. Anna Belle Jackson assisted in motivating some fifty-five National Convention women from fourteen states to attend. Fannie Blackburn from Second Christian Church, Indianapolis, Indiana, and Rosa Page Welch from South Side Christian Church, Chicago, Illinois, were among the principal speakers. Alberta Craggett from Avalon Christian Church, Los Angeles, California, was the author of the Quadrennial Assembly theme song, "Constrained by Love".

## STAFF INTERRELATIONS AND RESPONSIBILITIES

The staff work of Jackson, like that of her two program associates Webb and Evans, demonstrated the total necessity for cooperative effort in program planning and servicing congregations, states and areas. Throughout the 1950's National Convention staff became increasingly inter-locked with the Anglo-American church staff in the various United Christian Missionary Society departments and the other major church agencies as they served the National Convention annual session, held worker's conferences, led schools of mission, and worked with children and youth.

During the mid-1950's, the State and Home Missions Planning Council became the main arena for the denomination to develop program materials and update methodologies and goals. Each of the Convention staff persons was appointed to membership in one of its nine sections along with three to five other Convention leaders. The Executive Secretaries for each of the related UCMS departments expected the Convention staff to attend the scheduled departmental staff planning retreats.

National Convention staff attended the meetings of ecumenical bodies like the National Council of Churches and participated in those aspects which had a particular relationship to their responsibilities.

It seemed logical that when the National Convention's Restudy Commission under the chairmanship of Sere S. Myers, held its third meeting on October 29, 1956 at Indian Lake, Indiana, A. Dale Fiers, then President of the UCMS, supported Chairman Myers, President R. H. Peoples and Convention Executive Secretary E. J. Dickson in a call for basic definitions. The Commission embarked on a definition of staff work, trustee functions, and the philosophy of work between the various service agencies.

In a statement of background for the work of the Commission, Myers observed:

"The Convention, through the years, has provided fellowship, has served as a sounding board and a liaison between Brotherhood agencies... It took the role, more or less, as an advisory instrument until the reorganization of the Convention ten years ago."

Ten years ago the Convention was reorganized and launched a new program which included its membership on Brotherhood boards and agencies. This plan provided the Negro churches and their leaders with a cooperative way to give expression to many of the things they had talked about a long time. This plan has been at work ten years and the Convention has grown in number, interest, support, and in staff...

Charles Webb, Sr., however, had used a staff report to put his finger on one of the emerging difficulties. Webb said:   "We must look at the matter of increasing overlapping of staff responsibilities of the headquarter's staff, state society staffs, and national staff.  When they work together and plan separately, where is the base of responsibility?"[2]

A small National Convention staff of four persons was being torn in all directions by a multiplicity of responsibilities. A correction in the direction of the overall operation had to be made in order to avoid total collapse. The provision of that correction was the mandate, which had been given to the Restudy Commission of the Convention.

Soon after the 1957 Annual Session Director Webb accepted a call to become the senior minister at Park Manor Christian Church, in Chicago, Illinois. His departure required Emmett Dickson to assume Webb's responsibilities in an "acting capacity" as well as to be the Convention's Executive Secretary. That dual role was performed until the staff merger in 1959.

The National Christian Missionary Convention leadership had developed a noble vision of Christian ministry. They had assumed broad responsibilities for the stewardship of the Gospel mission. The first decade of experience in self-development and support provided rich experiences in churchmanship. Spiritual qualities of courageous faith necessary to be Disciples of Christ in the contemporary world were developing. By the dawn of the expansive 1950's they could look back in celebration to where they had been. They were now in a much better position to know where they had to go to fulfill the Master's mission.

## THE ROLE OF THE SOCIAL ACTION COMMISSION

A complete understanding of the movement toward merger of staff and program services must include a review of the contributions made by the National Convention's Social Action Commission.  Affiliation with the United Christian Missionary Society and establishing an official relationship with the International Convention meant more than opportunities to receive a few dollars in support of worthy goals. Additional benefits included the receipt of methods and tools for aiding in the struggle to reform the Church and apply the Gospel to its life and witness. Broader arenas were provided where the gifts of the Afro-American Church experience and other spiritual gifts could be shared.

The NCMC Social Action Committee was formed during the 1952 Annual Convention Session in Los Angeles, California. This marked the beginning of a sophistication by the NCMC in initiating social change within the major structures and systems of both church and society.

Prior to the formation of the Social Action Commission, the Convention heard an exhaustive report from a representative who attended an annual meeting of the Federal Council of Negro Churches. Since the headquarters of this organization was in Washington, D. C., the representative who usually gave the report to the annual session of the NCMC was either J. F. Whitefield, minister of Twelfth Street Christian Church in Washington, D. C. or his brother, C. L. Whitefield, minister of Mount Olive Christian Church in Baltimore, Maryland. The report endeavored to cover every aspect of African-American life in and was read with great fervor and conviction.

However, the formation of the Social Action Commission brought into play a new sophistication in social action promotion and style. This sophistication came through the aid of staff in the UCMS Department of Social Welfare who were assigned by the Executive Secretary to resource the NCMC's Social Action Committee. Executive Secretary Emmett Dickson, sensitive to the importance of this vehicle, took special care to aid the Convention president in making appointments to this Committee. Further, the Program Committee always made provision for the Committee to make major input before every annual session.

## SOCIAL ACTION ISSUES

The 1953 International Convention meeting in Portland, Oregon, adopted a resolution which committed the Convention to a policy of non-segregation in all sessions of the Convention, its constituent agencies, and in hotel and meal facilities. The NCMC Social Action Commission, in reporting this action to the National Convention, stated Convention (i. e. International) committees were "to press unremittingly for the full achievement of this policy at the earliest possible moment."

A ten-member Committee was appointed by the International Convention consisting of five members from the International Convention Executive Board and five members from the National Christian Missionary Convention to bring recommendations for implementation to Miami, Florida, in 1954.

Under the leadership of Chairman R. L. Jordan, minister of United Christian Church, Detroit, Michigan, and Department of Social Welfare Director Lewis Deer, the National Convention Social Action Commission had been instrumental in drafting the double-edged recommendation on implementation which was adopted by the National Convention and its essentials eventually approved by the Miami, Florida, International Convention. The "actions" proposed read:

"THEREFORE BE IT RESOLVED by this International Convention of Disciples of Christ in Convention Assembly at Miami, Florida, that all International Conventions be held in cities where there are adequate facilities in first-rate hotels and other places of meeting that are open to all participants without discrimination on account of race and color in such matters as Convention meeting places, hotel accommodations, room assignments and dining facilities,

"AND BE IT FURTHER RESOLVED that this resolution supersedes previous action on this subject and that it shall serve as a directive to the Time and Place Committee, and that the Recommendation Committee of the International Convention be advised at once of the approval of the National Convention of this resolution,

FURTHERMORE, we recommend that the Board of the National Convention and its Committee on Recommendations give serious study in the next year to this resolution in relation to its meaning for the National Convention."

This recommendation was "double-edged" because it not only called for the International Convention to take action but also the National Convention to make a serious, related response.

The Social Action Commission assisted the National Convention in monitoring the final commitment made by the International, and encouraged the National Convention membership to become full participants in the life and work of the International. Many of the agonizing moments of frustration and embarrassment which had come to many members of both races when meeting together for fellowship and church business would eventually be at an end.

An added boon for social reform came the following year on May 17, 1954, when the Supreme Court of the United States handed down what the Social Action Commission termed "the greatest decision this country has witnessed since the Emancipation Proclamation: the outlawing of segregation in our public schools..." The Commission further advised:

This decision goes farther than most of us realize. It outlaws segregation... It calls upon our brotherhood requesting our churches to instruct their members to meet this situation with patience and prayer... It also requests this Convention (NCMC) to encourage our churches to begin seminars to educate our people for the larger role we are called upon to play in our community life... We recommend that our Convention and its churches explore ways and means... while recognizing the peculiar nature, laws, and customs of the several sections of our country.[3]

As was customary, the Commission report went on to discuss: (a) the relationship of Christian morality and concern for issues of better morality in communities; (b) the need for greater number of community service-minded congregations; (c) the evils of alcohol and gambling; (d) atomic warfare and world peace; and (e) the worthiness of the mission of the United Nations.

But the main emphasis was on race relations on the home front. As an outgrowth of the various declarations by the International Convention and the prompting of the NCMC, the United Christian Missionary Society's Department of Social Welfare designed and sponsored a major "Conference on Desegregation," which took place in Cleveland, Ohio, in May 1955. The purpose was "to bring together leaders of our churches... at both congregational and agency levels...". Most ministers attending as representatives of the National Convention were impressed by the sincerity of the participants. One pastor returned to his predominantly African-American congregation to report that "the National Christian Missionary Convention was voted out of existence twice at the meeting."

In December 1955, Rosa Parks, a Montgomery, Alabama, seamstress with tired feet, refused to give her seat to an Anglo-American on the city bus. Four days later the famous bus boycott began. These were turbulent times.

Resources were developed by staff director Lewis Deer in the Department of Social Welfare for Social Education Conferences. Examples of these were the 1955 Cleveland event and the Interracial Consultations on Southern Churches and Race Relations held between 1959 and 1963. Studies of the racial composition of Disciples of Christ congregations were also available.

The table below on "Racial and Ethnic Composition in Disciples of Christ Congregations, 1955 - 1956" presents data underscoring the predominantly Anglo-American nature of the denomination's membership. During the Centennial Assembly of the International Convention of the Disciples of Christ in session at Cincinnati, Ohio, October 25-30, 1949, the representatives referred a resolution to the Department of Social Welfare that dealt with the "inclusion of all races in church membership." In 1950 the International Convention approved in substance racial integration at the congregational level and urged the churches to make this "the first goal of the new century." The Department, in cooperation with the Social Action Commission of the National Convention, worked diligently to motivate congregations to achieve this goal.

## TABLE 5

## RACIAL AND ETHNIC COMPOSITION IN
## DISCIPLES OF CHRIST CONGREGATIONS

| GROUP | CHURCHES | MEMBERS IN ETHNIC CHURCHES | MEMBERS IN CHURCHES 2 OR MORE RACES | TOTAL MEMBERS |
|---|---|---|---|---|
| Negro | 556 | 51,184 | 791 | 51,975 |
| Hispanic | 10 | 636 | 754 | 1,390 |
| Japanese | 2 | 256 | 753 | 1,009 |
| Puerto Rican | 4 | 382 | 18 | 400 |
| Indian | 1 | 52 | 433 | 485 |
| Chinese | 0 | 0 | 237 | 237 |
| Filipino | 1 | 74 | 18 | 92 |
| TOTAL | | | | |
| Non-White | 574 | 52,584 | 3,004 | 55,588 |
| Caucasian | 7,408 | | | 1,634,363 |

The above estimate is based on the 1956 YEAR BOOK figures for the membership of identifiable ethnic congregations, and the information from the 1955 survey of racial practices for the additional numbers of ethnic group that were reported in the membership of multi-racial churches.

The work of the Social Action Commission, then, was not only concerned with social issues within the secular community, but also meaningful reformation within the church. The two inter-twined. This was vividly illustrated in the Baltimore, Maryland, Annual Session in 1957. At the same time the Social Action Commission was making its report to the National Convention, a few miles away in Washington, D. C., the United States Congress was preparing to pass the historic Civil Rights Act.

It is also significant that some time before any department in the UCMC or any other church agency secured a professional African-American staff person, the Department of Social Welfare employed Thomas J. Griffin as a national director to resource social education and community action committees in congregations. Later Gerald Cunningham was employed with responsibilities for various aspects of race relations and social justice.

## ACTION WITHIN CHURCH AGENCY STRUCTURES: THE NATIONAL BENEVOLENT ASSOCIATION

A recurring floor debate in most International Convention Assemblies and business sessions of the National Convention between 1952 and 1962 dealt with the reluctance of the National Benevolent Association's central administration to make a definitive stand on racial integration homes and social service programs. Among the notable spokesman for the NBA taking a more creative and constructive stand were Kring Allen, minister of McCarty Memorial Christian Church, Los Angeles, California, and L. L. Dickerson, minister of Monroe Avenue Christian Church, Columbus, Ohio.

In the late 1930's and early 1940's the National Convention had given some consideration to the establishment of homes for African-American children and the aged. Consequently, during the "Crusade for a Christian World", designers of the financial aspects of the "Crusade" had placed these money goals into the program. At the end of the "Crusade", $33,587 was allocated for "service to the Negro aged, and $26,867 for service to Negro children...".

The idea of separate programs for African-American aged and children eventually lost favor, and the struggle continued to achieve a policy of total racial integration. However, in 1954, NBA administrative leadership persisted in promoting the idea of the separate approach. A full-page provocative advertisement which left a negative impression on most African-American Disciples of Christ was placed in the program book of the National Convention which convened in St. Louis, Missouri. The ad chastised Black Disciples of Christ in Alabama, California, Illinois, Missouri, North Carolina and Tennessee for giving only $73.25 to NBA during 1953-54. It rehearsed the history of the money being raised during the "Crusade for a Christian World" and allocated for social services to African-American aged and children and ended with a "Wonderful challenge before the Negro churches...to average at least one dollar-benevolent dollar per member per year for their (Black) Benevolent program to be launched and supported..." 3

More hot oil was added to the debate on NBA policy and little constructive results realized. Eventually some of the "Crusade" funds were channeled to needy aged through community service committees in Black Disciples of Christ congregations who screened applicants. But it remained for a substantial program to be developed.

Steady attention was given to urge the recruitment of racial and ethnic students and faculty by institutions of higher education, and the election of them to membership on the boards of all of the church agencies.

The Convention voted to provide money to enable the Social Action Commission to meet four times a year to develop strategies and program. In 1960 at the forty-fourth annual session of the NCMC at Woodland Avenue Christian Church, Columbus, Ohio, the Commission presented Roy Wilkins, Executive Secretary of the National Association for the Advancement of Colored People, New York City, as the principal speaker for "Social Action Night." The sit-in movement which had been initiated by four college students from North Carolina A. and T. College, Greensboro, North Carolina, in February was at its zenith. Summit conferences of national African-American leaders concerned about the elimination of racial segregation in all aspects of United States life were taking place.

An additional feature of the evening's program was special recognition of the following Disciples of Christ who had made significant contribution to civil rights and social justice during the year: Eugene Mason,

Montgomery, Alabama; L. L. Dickerson, Columbus, Ohio; Osceola Dawson, Paducah, Kentucky; Kring Allen, Los Angeles, California; Arthur A. Azlein, Washington, D. C.; Lois Marie Mothershed, Grace E. Mothershed, and Thelma J. Mothershed, of Little Rock, Arkansa; Mr. and Mrs. Paul Sims, Fort Worth, Texas.

The stage was set for the persons attending the National Convention that night to be on edge to hear the words of civil rights organization leader, Roy Wilkins, first-hand.

Such was the atmosphere within which the Convention's Re-Study (Merger of Program and Services) Commission began and launched its work. Thus, in addition to the very real administrative difficulties the Commission was trying to unsnarl, it also had to be forever sensitive to the tremendous social currents that were engulfing the whole of society during these years.

## CHAPTER NINE

# PHASE III. THE MERGER OF PROGRAM AND SERVICES (1955-1962)

The National Christian Missionary Convention's future is tied up with the future of our world. We are part and parcel of the world in which we live... Our Disciple heritage and plea for unity among God's people demand that we have one church and one Convention.
—*Robert Hayes Peoples, 1955*

The present goal we seek is to:

1. Share in the administration of Brotherhood agencies by being on policy-making boards and committees.

2. Share in the work and employment at all levels

3. Share in the drama and exhibition of the work of the church as performed by the organized life of the Brotherhood...

4. Share in the financial support of the causes and concerns of the church...(and)

5. Share faithfully and loyally in the activities, fellowship, and aspiration of the Brotherhood as we move toward complete integration.
—*Emmett J. Dickson, former executive secretary of NCMC, 1969*

R. H. Peoples resigned from his national field staff position in 1944 and become the pastor of Second Christian Church, Indianapolis, Indiana. He had given long and intensive thought to how the National Convention might merge staff and services as well as the two Conventions. Now as President of the National Convention in 1955, the time had come for him to share those insights with the Re-study Commission.

Early in the discussions, Dr. Peoples shared the vision of what he called "Proposed Plans for Merging the National Christian Missionary Convention with the International Convention of Disciples of Christ and the United Christian Missionary Society". The basic concept developed was the merging of the services and work of the NCMC with the services and work of both the International Convention and the UCMS.

The first aspect of the "plan" called for the National Convention to remain as a "fellowship-assembly" to promote an annual meeting for inspiration and education and maintain a legal corporation which could be a property-holding body. It would also serve as a means for relating African-American congregations to the rest of the church. The Executive Secretary was to be employed by the office of the International Convention and have the status of an Associate Executive Secretary. He or she would relate to the National Convention and maintain appropriate relationships to the International Convention and ecumenical groups.

The second part of Peoples' vision had to do with agency relations. Program development; related literature and related materials; sponsorship of training events; work with program planning bodies; and field services to congregations would be channeled through the United Society and other appropriate agencies. The three National Convention program directors would become full staff members of the appropriate UCMS departments. By virtue of their responsibilities, they would belong to one or more of the existing national program planning bodies (i. e. Curriculum Planning Council; Home and State Missions Planning Council; Field State Conference; Religious Education Association, or Christian Women's Fellowship).

After extensive time was spent evaluating Convention's operations and assessing and defining tasks, the Commission dealt with some of the aspects of the Peoples' proposal. A few months prior to the 1959 Annual Session in Dallas, Texas, the Commission—now called Merger of Program and Services—approved in principle and spirit, the following:

1.   The ultimate goal is to integrate the NCMC and its constituent churches into the total Brotherhood life.

2.  That the Assembly be maintained for fellowship.

3.  That the first step to achieve the ultimate goal would be to merge the program and services of the NCMC with the Brotherhood agencies responsible for such services.

The Trustees and Commission were authorized to present a detailed plan to the 1959 Dallas convention for carrying out those three objectives. The Commission Report on Merger of Program and Services was adopted during the Dallas Session and authorization was given to negotiate the following "Next Steps Toward Merger":

1.  The three program staff of the NCMC be transferred from the direct supervision of the NCMC to the staff of the UCMS and that those staff persons would maintain the same professional status and relationship as other staff members carrying similar portfolios;

2.  The UCMS be requested to maintain in its employ a minimum of four staff on an executive level;

3.  To insure that Negro churches receive the attention which is currently needed, the UCMS be requested to set up a staff committee including Black staff members to deal with problems that may arise in regard to program services growing out of the Merger;

4.  Black representatives selected as board members on the policy-making boards of all church agencies, especially the United Christian Missionary Society;

5.  The Council of Agencies, in cooperation with the NCMC, be asked to create an Interracial Commission for the purpose of furthering complete integration in such matters as:

    (a)     Securing representation on administrative boards;

    (b)     Securing employment for Negroes at all levels; and

    (c)     Securing opportunities to share in the drama and exhibition of the work of the church as performed in the organized life of the brotherhood organizational leadership, missionaries, officers, teachers, as well as sermons, papers, consultations, pictures, publications, recognitions, appeals, conventions, and agency participation in general.

6. A staff member of the UCMS Department of Social Welfare be provided to act as the Administrative Secretary of the Interracial Commission and financing come from the NCMC and cooperating agencies; and

7. The NCMC have an Executive Secretary outside of UCMS responsible to the Fellowship Assembly of the NCMC whose term would be four years and duties described by constitutional amendment.

The merger of staff and program services did not relieve the National Convention from major responsibilities. A tremendous task of interpretation and motivation of congregational leadership lay ahead and the Convention structure was vital. The following refinement of Convention Board functions were adopted:

1. Convention Board of Trustees would continue on a bi-racial basis and have its functions reviewed periodically.

2. Carry out the traditional responsibilities of:

    (a)    Serve as liaison between the constituency of he National Convention and other constituency groups of brotherhood life;

    (b)    Administer the permanent funds and property of the National Christian Missionary Convention;

    (c)    Sponsor the Annual Assembly of the constituency; and,

    (d)    Plan and administer, through its Executive, an annual budget.

A key hope of the planners of the merger of staff and services was for the Christian stewardship of time, abilities and money to be shared in greater abundance with the whole Church. It was anticipated that the bulk of assembly support of the Annual Session of NCMC would come from registrations. Further, there was earnest interest in increased financial giving by the NCMC congregations to Unified Promotion, which provided the funds for UCMS to pay the staff.

In June 1961, Willard Wickizer, the UCMS Executive Secretary of the Division of Church Life and Work, was pleased to report that since July

1, 1960, Emmett J. Dickson had been employed as National Director of Church Relations on the staff of the Division of Church Life and Work. Lorenzo J. Evans had been appointed National Director of Field Services in the Department of Christian Education. Following the resignation of Anna Belle Jackson, Carrie Dee Hancock was doing interim service until Lois Mothershed of Little Rock, Arkansas would begin full time on June 15, 1961. At that point, no one had been secured to fill the full portfolio once carried by Charles Webb, Sr.

In order to improve communications between the National Convention constituency and the United Society and related agencies, a Committee on Interim Developments in Negro Church Life had been created to alert the program departments to meet needs among predominantly African-American congregations.

Wickizer was also able to report that John R. Compton had become the first Black Trustee Board member of the United Christian Missionary Society. A few had been members of the Board of Managers, but not its Trustee Board. Emmett Dickson had been seated as a member of the UCMS Cabinet.

The merger of program and services was underway. But the Disciples of Christ, like every one else in Christendom, was heading into rising winds of social and cultural change that would radically change the priorities of mission at home as well as the manner in which they were to be achieved.

John Kennedy had defeated Richard Nixon for the presidency. Martin Luther King, Jr. was going from city to city laying his life on the line for human dignity and justice. Many Anglo-American ministers who advocated civil rights for African-Americans or got involved in activist civil rights demonstrations were fired from their pulpits. The Freedom Riders were using the means of public transportation across state lines to challenge the Jim Crow laws, which prevented Blacks from securing equal accommodations. And a riot occurred on the University of Georgia campus in Athens when African-American students, Charlayne Hunter and Hamilton Holmes were suspended by the institution.

The rising tide of the Civil Rights movement would strike the Church and all institutions until they would never be the same again.

# CHAPTER TEN

# PHASE IV: NEW DIRECTIONS FOR NEW TIMES (1960-1964)

"Ye have compassed (circled) this mountain long enough..."
says the Lord, "turn you northward"(Deuteronomy 2:3)
—*The Convention President's Message August 21, 1961*

The Negro baby born in America today regardless of the
section or state in which he is born has about one-half as much
chance of completing high school as a White baby born in
the same place on  the same day, one third as much chance
of completing college...twice as much chance as becoming
unemployed...
—*Emancipation Centennial Message to Congress, President John
Kennedy, 1963*

The mammoth March on Washington was a visible sign of
the potential... More than two hundred and fifty thousand
Americans- about sixty thousand of them White, participated
in the August 28, 1963 demonstration in Washington, D. C.
They came from points all over America and from several
overseas... They said with their bodies that Blacks had been
waiting 100 years and 240 days and they were still not free and
that 100 years and 241 days were too long to wait.
—*BEFORE THE MAYFLOWER by Lerone Bennett, Jr., 1982, p. 405*

The signs of the new times were all around the church as members
of the National Christian Missionary Convention gathered for the
forty-fourth Annual Session in Columbus, Ohio, August 22, 1960,

with Monroe Avenue Christian Church as host. Rosa Brown Bracey Haynes, one of the last living symbols of the courageous fathers and mothers who pioneered the founding of the Convention, had died one month before the Assembly. She had been elected to head the Christian Women's Fellowship and serve as Second Vice-president of the Convention. Poor health had prevented her from filling the duties of office.

Her forty-seven years of staff services had become a legend of adventurous Christian faith and witness among Black and White Disciples of Christ. Like the Moses of Old Testament Bible times, she had been allowed to come to the edge of the "promised land" and then slip into the great transition. President John R. Compton of Cincinnati, Ohio led the assembly in moments of silent tribute. And the Convention went on to address the new and challenging times at hand.

Many Black and White Disciples of Christ leaders in both Conventions (i.e. National and International) were dedicated to guiding the two bodies and they're supporting congregations toward the goal of racial integration.

The Commission on Merger had stated this commitment in the preamble to its report when it said:

Christian Churches (Disciples of Christ) have always held the firm conviction that the Church is one as Christ prayed, "That they all may be one." While this has been commonly applied to denominational divisions, our basic philosophy also affirms that there can be no wholeness if any segment is excluded because of culture, race, or national origin. The Church is the creation of our Lord and Savior, Jesus Christ, composed of all those who profess His name... (Acts 17)

Our government, the National Council of Churches of Christ, our International Convention of Christian Church (Disciples of Christ), and numerous denominations have all spoken against segregation because of race... With this great cloud of witnesses it becomes necessary for us to build a fellowship that reflects the oneness of the Church, the unity of the believers in Christ. "In Christ there is neither Jew nor Greek." (Romans 10:11-13, Galatians 3:27-28.)

As President of the National Convention, John R. Compton did an efficient job in leading the Board of Trustees, Merger Commission and National Convention congregations into an acceptance of the new merger principles of operations. New and improved tools were now available to the Convention for doing the work. Administrations, which followed, would be challenged to put new substance into the mission message of the National Convention in general and African-American Disciples of Christ in particular.

The strivings of the nation to come to grips with the tremendous issues being raised by the civil rights movement, plus the struggle of the National and International Conventions to find their true calling as part of the body of Christ, provided a climate for Disciples of Christ state and regional church organizations to deal courageously with the race issue.

During the forty-third Session of the National Convention, President Compton could announce that during the year the Black and White convention organizations in Kansas had merged into one. Furthermore, the Ohio Christian Missionary Society (White) and the Ohio Christian Missionary Convention (Black) had joined into one body May 22, 1960. A new body was born to be known as "The Ohio Society of Christian Churches (Disciples of Christ). The denomination was moving haltingly toward the supreme goal of wholeness.

## FULFILLING MERGER COMMITMENTS

Upon the election of William K. Fox, pastor of Centennial Christian Church, St. Louis, Missouri, as President at the 1960 Annual Session, he envisioned four realities, which confronted the Convention and its Board of Trustees. First, the reality of the merger of staff and services. Second, an amended constitution, which suggested a new look at the function and structure of the Convention. Third, new forces that were at work in the world and among the churches which made a re-evaluation of the role of the Convention and cooperating churches a "must". And fourth, the new mood of togetherness in responsible churchmanship which was evident within the Christian Church (Disciples of Christ).

There were missing links in the process of staff merger that could not be overlooked. The departure of Anna Belle Jones from the directorship of Christian Women's Fellowship and missionary groups, and the resignation of Charles H. Webb Sr., as Director of Evangelism and Church Development, weakened the capabilities of the Convention/ UCMS to serve congregations in those areas of church. Carrie Dee Hancock and Velma Dreese were co-opted to carry on some of Anna

Belle Jones' responsibilities. Emmett J. Dickson assumed some of the activities in Webb's former portfolio. But as dedicated as the interim staff was, the responsibilities were too broad and overwhelming.

One of the actions of the February 15-16, 1961 Board of Trustees urged, "The securing of Negro personnel as a part of the Department of Church Development to facilitate a more effective evangelism of the Negro churches during this period of transition".

Donald M. Salmon, Executive Secretary for the Department of Evangelism and his assistant, Russell A. Deitch, eventually attempted the sponsorship of special conferences on evangelism for a select number of National Convention pastors, but a sustained church-wide and successful program for African-Americans was non-existent.

Lorenzo Evans had been transferred to the Department of Christian Education. But the staff of D. Allison Holt, Executive Secretary of the Department of Christian Education, was grappling with a strategy on how to serve seven African-American youth conferences, six Chi-Rho camps, and two junior camps in the South. The only direct contact with an African-American conference or camp by any staff, besides Evans, was in the Piedmont Tri-State Area.

In addition to the challenges of making the plan for the merger of program and services work, the National Convention was confronted with serious difficulties in the administration of the Preston Taylor properties in Nashville, Tennessee and Greenwood Cemetery. The grand plan for developing the cemetery was not paying off. Personal and other reasons required the manager, Merle R. Eppse, to offer his resignation. The future of this important legacy from Preston Taylor was in jeopardy. Fortunately, L. L. Dickerson, who had recently accepted a call to serve Gay-Lea Christian Church of Nashville, Tennessee, was able to assume managerial responsibilities at Greenwood on an interim part-time basis.

Another management crisis occurred in the operation of the Taylor Memorial Fellowship House, which required the abandonment of the program and sale of the property. On February 20, 1961, money from the sale ($9,143.90) was deposited with the UCMS in the Negro Scholarship Fund. These funds increased the principle to be invested and brought earnings from which Star Supporter Scholarship grants to qualified students could be made. In the meantime, the United Christian Missionary Society, under the direction of Willard

Wickizer, had formed a "Program and Policy Committee on Interim Developments in Negro Church Life". In reporting this fact to the National Board Executive Secretary Emmett J. Dickson, he indicated that the Committee was "not an operative committee," but "recognizes needs and by specialized ministry tries...to help regular channels..." meet those needs.

The Committee was not an inter-agency committee, but membership on the Committee came from the United Christian Missionary Society, Board of Higher Education, Christian Board of Publication, Unified Promotion, and the National Christian Missionary Convention. It was originally designed to meet twice a year until the merger process had been fully realized.

Soon after the merger of UCMS and Convention staffs serving predominantly African-American congregations was formally realized, they were provided important research data which helped clarify the nature of the emerging mission challenge. First, Carrie Dee Hancock, who had become the interim worker in the place once held by Anna Belle Jones, began a one-on-one field visitation of Black congregations and their leadership. With the assistance of staff members like D. Allison Holt and Lorenzo J. Evans, who joined her in the visitations, a fresh picture of problems confronting Convention congregations was surfacing monthly.

By December 20, 1960, the time of the first meeting of the Program and Policy National Committee, Convention related congregations had been visited in Kentucky, Eastern Tennessee and Ohio. An orientation to the life and work of UCMS had been given to each church and general questionnaires on the congregations were filled out. Information from the questionnaires was shared with the respective state society staffs and departments of UCMS. The project not only provided updated information on the nature of service needs existing among these congregations, but also helped to cement relationships and develop understanding and appreciation between congregations, A. Dale Fiers, the UCMS President, and the staffs in related state societies.

Soon after the Carrie Dee Hancock Visitation Project, Dale W. Medaris produced the 1961 YEAR BOOK STUDY OF CHRISTIANN CHURCHES (DISCIPLES OF CHRIST) with the assistance of Franklin E. Rector at Christian Theological Seminary, Indianapolis, Indiana. The study included 544 predominantly African-American congregations. That data underscored much that was seen first-hand by those doing the Hancock field visitations or known and experienced by African-American staff who had served National Convention congregations for several years.

The Medaris study indicated: (a) a reluctance on the part of Black congregations to turn in YEAR BOOK reports; (b) a predominance of small congregations in rural areas; and (c) a limited sharing of finances with the total church mission effort. This financial sharing came mainly from urban congregations.

Other data on church schools, fellowship groups and finance helped to accent a picture of program and staff service needs. Together the Hancock and Medaris investigations outlined a call for services unsurpassed in challenge.

In 1961, the forty-fifth Annual Session of the Convention in Brooklyn, New York, was launched by President Fox with a ringing message on "New Directions for New Times". He spoke from the text found in Deuteronomy 2:3, which says: "Ye have compassed this mountain long enough...turn northward". The Convention was paralleled to the Hebrew children. The President claimed it was time to stop going in circles. He challenged the body to move "northward" (forward) in the following "New Directions for New Times" by:

1.  Being more than a mere fellowship convention group toward being a remnant of redemption;

2.  Moving away from a fixation on things structural and material toward an emphasis on demonstrations in the dynamics of the spirit;

3.  Going toward an unashamed alliance of the Christian Church with all worthy efforts to secure full citizenship rights and responsibilities for all people on the one hand, and toward an appreciation for the heritage of American Negroes and the part they play in the enrichment of world culture; and,

4.  Moving away from minimum membership in the local church to a larger participation in the expansion of the kingdom of God through a united church.

The President's address provided a number of specifics as to how these "new directions for new times" might be achieved and aroused the interest of many conventioneers and leaders. Using the delivery styles of both sermon and address, he: (a) had outlined the history and struggle of the Convention from its inception to the merger of staff and services; (b) was critical of its indecision; and (c) challenged "at least 200 churches, church schools, fellowship groups and auxiliaries to" inner spiritual re-vitalization.

The church representatives were challenged to perform actions of courageous faith and reconciliation in keeping with the needs of the new times. They were reminded of the faith of the early Convention fathers and mothers and encouraged to make alignment with other Black Christian bodies and movements to achieve full Christian citizenship.

## LIVING OUT THE FIVE-FOLD SHARING FORMULA

The National Convention was going through a difficult time of interpreting its fundamental purpose and role to the related congregations as well as service agencies. The five-fold sharing formula which had been first presented to the 1959 annual session of the National Convention in Dallas, Texas, gave some guidelines. Executive Secretary Dickson and President Fox began work on the sharing "in the drama and exhibition" principle by meeting with the Program Committee of the International Convention on October 12, 1961. They recommended Walter D. Bingham of Louisville, Kentucky, and Peter Washington of Berkeley, California, to be considered for major addresses. E. W. Henry, Jr. of Los Angeles, California; R. H. Peoples of Indianapolis, Indiana; R. L. Saunders of Brooklyn, New York; and K. David Cole of Oklahoma City, Oklahoma, were proposed as worship leaders or as "participants in buzz or interest group structures...".

When the International Convention of Christian Churches (Disciples of Christ) met in Los Angeles, California, September 30-October 4, 1962, Walter D. Bingham brought the Tuesday afternoon sermon. Among other African-Americans who shared in the International Convention's operations was Martha W. Faw, a Public Relations Associate at Jarvis Christian College, who served on the Convention's Program Committee.

Work on interpretation continued in Indianapolis, Indiana, Thanksgiving weekend of November 24-25, 1961. Convention Executive Emmett J. Dickson called a "consultative conference" for the presidents of state conventions, state society secretaries, agency representatives and the National Convention to design an "expanded Fall Planning Conference concerned with each functional area of the church instead of only Christian education." Explanations on how to make the merger of program and services was also high on the agenda. Emmett J. Dickson was Moderator with some twenty-nine persons representing the various groups attending.[1]

E. W. James, Sr. of Roanoke, Virginia; A. J. Jeffries of Birmingham, Alabama; and Ozark Range, Sr. of Columbus, Ohio, formed a panel moderated by W. K. Fox, Sr. on "Where Do We Go From Here?". The job of communicating the story of change would continue to be a large responsibility. It became increasingly clear that Executive Secretary Dickson would need to initiate orientation meetings with state societies and African-American state convention leadership where on site interpretation could be given. Such was the advice and counsel, which eventually came from the Program and Policy Committee on Interim Developments in Negro Church Life.

Leaders were urged to call for help only when what they were doing required assistance. They were cautioned against asking a professional staff person to do for them what they could best do for themselves.

## OTHER CHURCH AGENCIES

Initially the merger concept was mainly a development between the National Convention and the United Christian Missionary Society. UCMS had a long history of relationships. At the same time there had been a growing relationship with the Christian Board of Publication through the printing of THE CHRISTIAN PLEA and eventually the establishment of a part-time editorial relationship. Further, Christian Board maintained an abiding interest in having more of the National Convention congregation using its curriculum and general church material. A large exhibit of contemporary books and general materials with accompanying personnel was provided for every annual session of the National Christian Missionary Convention.

In 1962, Christian Board of Publication expanded its interest in National Convention concerns by making a $15,000 grant to Jarvis Christian College. According to the publishing house President Wilbur H. Cramblet, it was a grant-in-aid distributed over a three-year period. In acknowledging the grant, Executive President J. O. Perpener indicated that it would be used to help provide a library and classroom facilities necessary to serve a growing student body and for the college to receive accreditation from the Southern Association of Colleges.

Another agency to develop meaningful staff relationships with predominantly African-American congregations having ties to the National Convention, was the Board of Church Extension. In the early 1960's, BCE developed a practice of enlisting architectural and program consultants who were "on call." The Board provided expenses and a per diem for services rendered. The Board of Directors established a policy to do intentional recruitment of African-American professionals who could serve as "consultant staff" on call. This practice eventually led to the full-time employment of Raymond E. Brown of Hannibal, Missouri, as a consultant. This step led to the Board's employment of clerical and technical staff. There was a liberalization of loan policies and guidelines in providing services to congregations—especially those who were predominantly African-American or Hispanic. A vast untapped resource for staff services was opened to the Board and mutual benefits derived for all concerned. At this point in time, no other Disciples of Christ agency—outside of UCMS—had been so intentional in its employment practices and provision of staff services to racial/ethnic congregations.

In his final address to the National Convention meeting August 20-26, 1962, in Brooklyn, New York, with the Williamsburg Christian Church as host, President Fox reminded those attending:

All over the world black men are struggling from under the weight and crippling of paternalism. They want to stand on their own feet and assume responsibilities like other men. They want to have failure and success like the rest of humankind. They know that if black men are to remain forever strapped to the backs of their white brothers they will never have enough bone tissue to stand up and walk like true men of God. If the end result of racial integration in the Church is the development of milk-fed Negro Christians, let us have no racial integration.

Racial integration in the Church must not become an avenue by which Negro churchmen avoid their divine responsibility to become mature Christians.

Through an initiative of the Convention's Social Action Commission, Jackie Robinson, the first African-American baseball player to break into the major leagues, brought the keynote address. Robinson claimed "No Negro has `made it' until the most underprivileged Negro in the country has `made it.'". During the session a student, an insurance man and a minister were given "Freedom Fighter Awards" for the parts they played in campaigns to open public facilities to Blacks in the South.

A resolution on Segregation in Brotherhood Colleges was adopted asking Atlantic Christian College in Wilson, North Carolina; Christian College of Georgia at Athens, Georgia; Lynchburg College, Lynchburg, Virginia; Texas Christian University, Fort Worth, Texas; and the Disciples Divinity House at Vanderbilt University, Nashville, Tennessee, to "take immediate steps to open their doors to all qualified students without regard to race."

## EMPHASIS ON "THIS MINISTRY"

During World War II, the Minister's Fellowship of the Convention had played a key role in the general programming of the Annual Session. The Fellowship usually chose the morning Bible lecturer and supplied the honorarium, for example. Following the rift with the "Baltimore" Taylor group of ministers, there was pressure to have more preaching in the regular program.

The program planners for the 1962 Session in Brooklyn, New York, accepted a recommendation from the Minister's Fellowship to have a "Pentecostal Preaching Service" on Tuesday morning. There was a series of sermons by six ministers (i.e. T. R. Moore, Little Rock, Arkansas; S. J. Compton, Dallas, Texas; Bishop W. M. Johnson, Brooklyn, New York; Claude Walker, Nashville, Tennessee; Augusta Burke, San Antonio, Texas; and Jesse J. Hawkins, Des Moines, Iowa). Ministers led the prayers and shared in the leadership of music. This lifted up the preaching ministry before the entire Convention.

But a more fundamental emphasis on ministry came through the Convention's Commission on "This Ministry" which received broad-scale support. Its purpose was to assist in the encouragement of ministers to complete the college liberal arts courses and seminary work in theology necessary to receive the prevailing ministerial degrees. In addition to relating to the promotion of the Star Supporter Fund and having representation on the Scholarship Committee, it endeavored to promote general well being and interest in an adequately prepared ministry.

It was within this general interest that in 1960 the Commission, under the chairmanship of John Compton, pressed for, "an exhaustive and comprehensive study of our church-related institutions of higher learning with regard to academic standing and accreditation by regional agencies and the American Association of Theological Schools, policy of admission, educational program...and ways and means to cooperate with the administrations of these schools in the training of our ministers".[2]

This was an ambitious vision for the Commission that was not readily achievable. Little movement was made in 1960-61 toward getting such a study accomplished.

At the forty-sixth Session of the National Convention in Brooklyn, New York, the Commission, under the chairmanship of William H. Brown of Georgia, came back with a comprehensive report covering all aspects of the quest for an adequately prepared African-American ministry. An able bodied Commission including lay leaders William H. Elster of Louisville, Kentucky; Norman S. Ellington, St. Louis, Missouri; Ozark Range, Columbus, Ohio; Jesse Hawkins, Hawkins, Texas; and five UCMS staff headed by Thomas Wood, the Director of the Department of Ministerial Services, had worked hard on the contents.

The Commission members felt that it needed to be given status—that is: (a) full recognition as a Commission with an operating budget; and (b) "tenure"—meaning "a continuation of membership that will allow continuity and knowledge..." of the Commission and its work.

The Commission had reviewed findings from a consultation, which had been held in Texas during 1962 on "The Ministry to Minority Groups." It contained a compilation of facts from surveys and studies of racial/ethnic ministers by A. C. Cuppy and William K. Fox. The Commission on "This Ministry" believed that only a unit like the Commission could deal effectively with such matters as (a) the changing African-American church; (b) the changing image of ministry for the changing church; (c) the large number of aged and untrained ministers; and the insufficient number of professionally competent Black ministers available to fill the new openings in a variety of church vocations.[3]

## SCHOLARSHIP SUPPORT

Interest among the congregations in providing scholarships for those preparing for full-time Christian vocations was on the upswing. A. C. Stone, National Promotional Agent for the Star Supporter Fund, announced that contributions at the Brooklyn session had passed all previous totals. Eight students were to receive scholarships to attend seminaries and four who attending college. The 1962-1963 money goal was to be $4,000.

Promotional enthusiasm was kept high through the use of traveling trophies.    The Kentucky Christian Men's Fellowship, under the leadership of promoters Buford Hall and Charles P. Sizemore, received the state trophy for the third straight year and retired the award. Second Christian Church of Hannibal, Missouri, under the leadership of CMF president James P. Griggsby and its pastor, Raymond E. Brown, received the local church trophy for the third straight year, and thus was given permanent ownership. The Star Supporter Fund had become a meaningful challenge to the men's organization of the church.

## CONVENTION SCHOLARSHIP COMMITTEE

A companion factor in the emphasis upon a prepared ministry was the work of the Scholarship Committee. One of the relationships that was expanded when the merger of program and staff services was put in motion was the relationship to the Office of Ministerial Services in the Department of Church Development. This office had always tried to resource the Minister's Fellowship of the Convention in a variety of ways. However, when the merger of staff services occurred it took on the task of keeping records on the various scholarship funds. UCMS staff became the chair of the Committee.

As long as funds in earnings from the Negro Scholarship Trust Fund remained, the Scholarship Committee gave grants to any Black Disciples of Christ student having financial need and seeking higher education in an accredited institution.   However, those who indicated a desire to enter the ministry and/or church vocations were given preference.

Star Supporter funds and the scholarship money raised annually by the Convention Minister's Wives' Fellowship went to the Negro Scholarship Trust Fund and was designated to help ministerial students.

Earnings from the SCI Alumni Scholarship Fund provided scholarships for Tougaloo (Mississippi) College students.  This was regarded as one way to give meaning to the 1954 merger of Southern Christian Institute with Tougaloo College.  The scholarships had no specific relationship to a student preparing for full-time professional Christian service.

There was also a Tougaloo Scholarship Fund initiated with $50,000 from the sale of Southern Christian Institute.  This was administered by the Department of Mission Ministries of the UCMS. However, these earnings went into special program projects directed toward Black Disciples of Christ and selected annually by a UCMS staff committee.

The impressive world mission tours of Rosa Page Welch had prompted the formation of a Rosa Page Welch Scholarship Fund with earnings initially administered by the World Division's Department of Missionary Selection and Training. They were to help provide scholarships for foreign missionary candidates.

The work of the Convention's Scholarship Committee was eventually coordinated in 1962 under the chairmanship of Staff Director Thomas E. Wood. It became known as "The Scholarship Committee of the Negro Scholarship Fund of the National Christian Missionary Convention and the United Christian Missionary Society." Its main sources of income came from CMF Star Supporter Funds, interest earnings, the Minister's Wives' Fellowship, and miscellaneous receipts.

But the Convention's Commission on "This Ministry" wanted greater focus on a prepared ministry. They deplored the "shot-gun" methods of recruitment, which seemed to have been used most frequently. They declared the standards of living and the "new image" of the Negro was presenting the church with the challenge of developing a stronger pulpit ministry.

## CHAPTER ELEVEN

# PHASE V: CONFRONTING MERGER REALITIES AND THE CONTEMPORARY SECULAR SCENE (1963-1966)

...the day-to-day lot of the rural Negro of the South or the ghetto Negro of the North has not been measurably improved by all the judicial and legislative measures of the past decade. In spite of innumerable meetings, marches, and martyrdoms, in spite of countless arrests, beatings and other forms of brutality endured, in spite of all the blood, sweat, and tears poured out, the day-by-day life of the average Negro in Mississippi or Manhattan, Selma, or Chicago, Atlanta or Louisiana has not been affected. This is the brutal reality that has created such bitter disappointment among Negroes...
—*BLACK POWER by George A.Chauncey, February 1967, in Church and Society, Presbyterian Church, U. S.*

1.   Our Convention churches need inspiration and fellowship...

2.   Negro Disciples need to feel a common bond with other Negro church bodies...

3.   Negro Disciples need a channel through which interpretation of cultural change, creative protest    and    general    expression can be made on matters of church development in the Negro community...
—*The preamble to the first report of the Special Committee on Study and Re-evaluation Detroit, Michigan, August 1963*

The "Black Manifesto" has been put before the churches, including thereby the Christian Church (Disciples of Christ). It cannot be ignored.  It reflects an anguish that we share,

arising from the gross abuse of minority groups in our land. It confronts us with the deep sickness of the spirit which characterizes our common life and which threatens the democratic institutions and processes of our society...
—*The preamble to Resolution No. 19 of the International Convention: "A Message from the General Board to the Christian Church (Disciples of Christ), August 15, 1969*

Charles H. Webb, Sr., minister at Park Manor Christian Church, Chicago, Illinois, and former Convention field staff, assumed the presidency of the National body in 1963. It was a year destined to be of high moment and significance in the history of the nation and the world.

It was the Emancipation Proclamation Centennial Celebration year with the National Association for the Advancement of Colored People announcing an ambitious legislative program to wipe out the last vestiges of legalized racial segregation in the land. Unfortunately, President Webb's wife, Margarette, died during the first four months of his administration. This affected his ability to supply vigorous leadership for both his ministry at Park Manor Christian Church in Chicago, Ilinois, and the National Convention.

U. S. President John F. Kennedy was assassinated in Dallas, Texas. A few hours before, Granville T. Walker, minister University Christian Church in Fort Forth, Texas, had heard the President speak at a Fort Worth breakfast, and changed his plan to read a scripture as the benediction and wrote a special prayer instead. The whole country and the world were saddened by this unforgettable tragedy.[1]

When the One Hundred Fourteenth Assembly of the International Convention convened in Miami, Florida, October 11-16, 1963, more than 6,000 representatives in attendance voted for strong stands on civil rights and Christian unity. James Farmer, director of the Congress of Racial Equality, spoke during the Miami meeting commemorating the one-hundredth anniversary of the Emancipation Proclamation. And a resolution was passed approving the International Convention's board action to create a Coordinating Committee on Moral and Civil Rights. The endorsement included a request for special offerings of at least $300,000 to finance the new civil rights thrust of the church.

J. Irwin Miller of Columbus, Indiana, the first lay person to serve as President of the National Council of Churches, introduced an "Act of Commitment" card for Miami convention-goers to register their intention to work for "an integrated church in an integrated society".

Zelma George of Cleveland, Ohio, who later wed Baxter Duke, minister of Avalon Avenue Christian Church, Los Angeles, California, delivered a major message at the Miami Convention affirming the role of the United Nations. She held that "the highest patriotism of any man anywhere is to help his country to play a worthy, creative and steadfast part in the United Nations and among the nations of the world..."

That year during United Nations Week, Ralph J. Bunche was the principle speaker and resource person at Tougaloo Southern Christian College, Disciples of Christ and the various church organizations relating to the National Christian Missionary Convention were struggling to respond to the ongoing social revolution.

It is understandable that against the backdrop of these turbulent social currents, the program emphases during the 1963 Annual Session of the NCMC were all related in some fashion to the rising tide of the Civil Rights movement. Second Christian Church of Rockford, Illinois, and its pastor, Daniel W. Heath, took a page from Williamsburg Christian Church of Brooklyn, New York, on hostmanship. It offered convention-goers the option of hotel accommodations as well the privilege of staying in homes. This was a departure from previous practice. But it was in keeping with the clamor of the hour for having access to equal public accommodations.

Under the leadership of the Commission on Social Action, the Convention program included a "Freedom Rally." "Testimonials of the Revolution" were given during a period called "Christian Citizens in Action." A. Garnett Day, who had just been employed as Program Coordinator for the Committee on Moral and Civil Rights, made a presentation in a morning plenary session. And A. Dale Fiers, who was serving as both Executive Secretary of the International Convention and Administrative Secretary of the Commission on Brotherhood Restructure, gave a significant address on "Next Steps in Restructure" during a period which considered the topic "Commission on Brotherhood Restructure Faces the Convention."[2]

The Special Committee on Re-Study and Re-evaluation pressed hard for an early consummation of the merger process which, in their judgment, would end with some sort of peer relationship to other agencies and organizations and the International Convention. The current civil rights revolution and its advocacy of racial solidarity in the face of overt oppression, strengthened the rationale to maintain the National Convention operation in some format at least as a place for gathering and reinforcement in the continuing struggle—both in the church and the world. This was the thinking of a Committee whose members included John R. Compton, L. L. Dickerson, William K. Fox, Sr., Blair T. Hunt, Robert L. Jordan, S.S. Meyers, and Robert H. Peoples.

They envisioned an "abbreviated National Assembly held at the same place prior to the International Convention" which would constitute another "step toward merger." They asked for a full-time Administrative Secretary who would "accelerate the implementation of the merger program".

Several lay leaders were eager to stimulate the mind of the Convention toward additional matters of substance, which would have a potential for provoking a basic change in the organization's direction. They communicated this concern to former Convention President William K. Fox, and asked him to be their speaker. Fox had been thinking seriously about the Convention's dilemma in mission and purpose. He was having new experiences in churchmanship and receiving new insights on Christian mission while working for a Metropolitan Church Federation in Indianapolis as a researcher and planner. He was about to move to New Jersey and serve as an executive staff member of the New Jersey Council of Churches. Fox accepted the invitation to speak to the Rockford, Illinois, session of the National Convention.

He brought a message entitled "Design for Renewal and Growth". Fox called for a "rebirth of spirit," a "rededication to mission," and a "realignment to God through a reaffirmation of Christ's lordship." These emphases were supported with specific references to "rebirth of Spirit" in the day-to-day operations of a congregation and its minister, the opportunities in the cities to reach the "unwanted, unevangelized, and untouched...," and the many visible blessings in mission victories in lives won to Christ, money given for the work, and new resources for the church discovered if Christ's lordship was sincerely affirmed.

This address prompted the Convention to develop a resolution called "Design for Renewal and Growth of the Christian Church (Disciples of Christ) Among Negroes." The resolution allotted $2,500 for a select Committee on Program and Structure to meet and work on the details.

Its mandate was to: ...work within the framework of the Brotherhood to bring new life into the National Convention churches. It was expected to develop philosophy, initiate strategy, and to stimulate the coordination of resources, which could result in better churches, more Disciples, more youth enlisting in church vocations and a more meaningful witness of the church to the urban ghetto.

The Committee brought in a variety of Disciples of Christ program staff and church consultants to dialogue with the Committee and share their insights and materials. After two years of exhaustive study and evaluation, the Committee presented a major report document, which was distributed to all program agencies and National Convention congregations.

The preface to the final report cited three socio-historical forces that were affecting the growth of the Disciples of Christ among African-Americans. These forces were:

1.  The sometimes conscious and at other times unconscious factors of paternalism... which gives evidence of being on the wane...

2.  The rise of the civil rights movement of the late 1950's and the early 1960's and its consequent stimulation of conscience among Caucasian Protestants and its pointing the way toward new possibilities for human dignity and social acceptance by White Americans and the corresponding new responsibilities which must be assumed by Negroes.

3.  The intensified struggle among Negro constituents in a church like the Christian Church (Disciples of Christ) to maintain their necessary racial and cultural identities, while at the same time finding new and significant roles in the ever-widening ecclesiastic relationships.[3]

The body of the report was written by designated Committee members. It outlined program goals and strategies in evangelism, church establishment and development, Christian education materials and methods, recruitment of ministers, and state and national organizational relationships. The study became an important program resource for several of the agency staffs in the national as well as state society offices largely because those staffs had a part in developing its contents.

## CHAPTER TWELVE

# PHASE VI: LED BY THE SPIRIT (1965-1969)

We realize that neither the term "power" nor the term "Christian Conscience" are easy matters to talk about... The fundamental distortion facing us in the controversy about "Black power" is rooted in a gross imbalance of power and conscience between Negroes and White Americans. It is this distortion, mainly, which is responsible for the widespread, though often inarticulate, assumption that White people are justified in getting what they want through the use of power, but that Negro Americans must, either by nature or circumstances, make their appeal only through conscience. As a result the power of White men and the conscience of Black men have both been corrupted. The power of White men is corrupted because it meets little meaningful resistance from Negroes to temper it and keep White men from aping God. The conscience of Black men is corrupted because, having no power to implement the demands of conscience, the concern for justice is transmuted into a distorted form of love, which, in the absence of justice, becomes chaotic self-surrender. Powerlessness breeds a race of beggars....
—*The preamble to BLACK POWER statement by the National Committee of Negro Churchmen, NEW YORK TIMES, Sunday July 31, 1966, section E, p.5.*

We affirm the Christian principle of reconciliation in dealing with alienation and evil. We declare our discipleship to our Lord who rated obedience to God's demand for justice a higher religious value than even the regular forms of worship and who urged his followers "first be reconciled with your brother." —*The Preamble to General Assembly Resolution No. 19 "A MESSAGE FROM THE GENERAL BOARD TO THE CHRISTIAN CHURCH (DISCIPLES OF CHRIST)", 1969, p. 104.*

The "Golden Anniversary" Session of the National Convention adopted the appropriate theme of "Led by the Spirit." Indeed, it was the tremendous spirit of social and civil revolution going on in the streets, courts and the neighborhoods which unquestionably affected the discussions the Convention's Committee on Program and Structure were having. Many African-American and Anglo-American Disciples of Christ were deeply involved in the happenings so visible daily on the television screen or seen easily in the newspaper and magazine headlines.

Out of the discussions of Program and Structure, which produced the "Design for Renewal and Growth", interest was expressed for a merger of all National Convention structures. Further, conversations on organizational relationships were not only going on between the National Convention and the International Convention, but restructure was being considered throughout the denomination. Thus, a Joint Committee on Merger and New Brotherhood Relations was formed in January 1966 for the expressed purpose of getting the two conventions together.

The joint committee had five members from the NCMC, five from the UCMS, and five from the International Convention. The final goal of their work together was expressed in the following commitment agreed upon in a July 1966 meeting:

In recognition that the ultimate unity of the International Convention of the Christian Church (Disciples of Christ) and the National Christian Missionary Convention is our essential purpose, we recommend to the International Convention of the Christian church (Disciples of Christ), the United Christian Missionary Society and the National Christian Missionary Convention the following:

1.  That all business procedures of the NCMC move to unification with the International Convention of the Christian Churches by 1968; however,

2.  That other functions vested in the present annual gathering of the NCMC shall continue under a new name, such as, National Christian Missionary Fellowship;

3.  For the purposes of fellowship of program service and development; and that the newly named organization (NCMF) meet biennially on years other than those years that the ICCC (DC) or its successor, hold its General Assembly.[1]

The mood of the moment in African-American communities and churches across the country was Black empowerment and self-determination. Thus there was much discussion of the issues raised by the members of the Joint Committee. Some advocated an open debate in order to safeguard the unity of the Fellowship. Others felt it was a waste of time. After extended discussion, the report of the Joint Committee was accepted by the Board of the National Convention as a "progress report," and instruction was given for the Committee to further work on the proposal and bring it to the next Annual Session of the National Convention. There remained considerable interest in "safeguarding the concerns of the Convention in the merger process."

But the Church was not totally without knowledge of the mind and desires of African-American Disciples of Christ. The "Design for Renewal and Growth" had been put in booklet form and widely distributed. At the same time there was a growing awareness on the part of Black Disciples leadership that some of the initiative for improving conditions in the Black church rested with their own congregations. The goal of racial integration had been the overriding vision originally, but the lessons of the current social revolution were putting emphasis on racial empowerment and pride.

The NCMC Committee on Program and Structure proposed some guidelines to the agencies and congregations for implementing "The Design for Renewal and Growth" in July 1967. Besides suggesting the development of orientation brochures to be sent to congregations, it was advised that agency boards make the report an official agenda item for review and response. National Convention "liaison agents" were to be co-opted to attend board meetings as interpreters and resources for implementation.

The guidelines also included a proposal for a "Capital and Program" Funds drive to culminate in August 1969. Such a drive was to point "toward securing money for ...National Christian Missionary

Convention churches... and be initiated by the National Convention in cooperation with the Board of Church Extension and Unified Promotion with appropriate counsel from program agencies."

The capital funding effort was to undergird specific program goals such as the following between 1970 and 1975:

*   Renewal of ten existing churches per year;

*   Construction of ten new churches per year;

*   Development of one new creative witness per year; and

*   Recruitment of seven young people per year for church vocations.

The guidelines also suggested an initiation of conversations with other church bodies like the Episcopal Church, United Presbyterian Church, American Baptist Church and the United Church of Christ. These churches were making similar efforts and might share experiences and insights.

## REVOLUTION IN THE CITIES

In the summer of 1967, while mainline Protestants like the Christian Church (Disciples of Christ) were developing measured and rational approaches to issues raised by a "Design for the Renewal and Growth of the Disciples of Christ Among Negroes in the U. S. A.," cities like Newark, New Jersey, had social explosions. God spoke in the fire, the whirlwind and the storm in olden times.  That summer a message came ringing unmistakenly clear through acts of rebellion and cries of agonizing frustration from militants as well as thoughtful suggestions by moderates that it was time for drastic change.

In Newark, New Jersey, the first National Black Conference had been held with the blessing of the Episcopal diocese.  The Church, at best, was a helpless spectator feverishly moving on the periphery of events in vain attempts to make incarnate its concern for human decency and change.

The rebellions in places like Newark, and New Brunswick, New Jersey; the Roxbury section of Boston, Massachusetts; Tampa, Florida; Cairo, Illinois; Memphis, Tennessee; and Cincinnati, Ohio, were the tips of vast icebergs of social unrest.  They came on the threshold of Richard L. Saunders' administration as President of the National Christian Missionary Convention. President Saunders supported the chairman of the Convention's Committee on Program and Structure in calling African-American Disciples of Christ ministers and selected leaders to a "survival" caucus meeting in Cincinnati, Ohio, June 26, 1968.

The "call" stated that the:

Cincinnati confab can not be just another meeting! It must become a "Family Gathering" - this means a Black Caucus in the truest sense! Black Disciples must meet by themselves to engage in the excruciating task of thinking Black, feeling Black and acting Black - not only for Black Disciple's sake, but for the sake of all of our brothers.[2]

In essence this was to be a Black strategy meeting with the agenda items oriented toward the contemporary churchmanship concerns as well as the civil rights revolution. Most responses made to the Program and Structure chairman and Convention President were supportive in the overall goals for the confab. However, some African-American Disciples of Christ ministers were hesitant to make such an approach.

A revered and respected Jason M. Cowan, then Associate Minister at United Christian Church, Los Angeles, California, wrote:

Dear Reverend Fox:

"...your recent "Open Letter of Call and Challenge... was alarming ...I.. expect to remain a part of the Christian Church (Disciples of Christ), which is color blind regardless of the succeeding and infinite sequences of change... My contacts with churches from Pennsylvania to California over some thirty-five years have confirmed a conviction that our "colorless brethren" are basically decent, and we need only to continue working, praying and forgiving. Together we shall become worthy to be called Christians.... Refrain from disturbing the Cincinnati, the Hawkins, and the Kansas City meetings with this divisive theory of "blackness,"..." (from June 18, 1968 letter)

Nearly 100 persons came to United Christian Church in Cincinnati, Ohio, for what was called a "Depth Conference of the National Christian Missionary Convention Ministers." Thomas Morris was the host pastor. The format for the two-day conference included a "Why We Are Here" statement by Convention Executive Secretary Emmett J. Dickson, a keynote message by President R. L. Saunders and a presentation on "The

Whole Church—Merger" by Kenneth Teegarden, Assistant to the General Minister and President, A. Dale Fiers. S.S. Myers served as convener.

The afternoon and evening sessions were so designed to get at the gut issues of the contemporary social crisis and "The Challenge of Black Disciples in White Church Structures." These concerns were approached from the standpoint of the "Preacher's Role in Today's World." Task groups were organized, invigorating discussion and suggested strategies registered. The event provided additional input for merger proceedings as well as the church-wide concern for meeting the challenge of the burning cities.

## THE CHURCH GIVES BIRTH TO QUINTUPLETS

Giving birth to quintuplets usually is front-page headline news. This is what the Christian Church (Disciples of Christ) did between 1968 and 1971. It strove to be faithful to its discipleship of Christ during these unusual times by being actively engaged in Christian action on at least five fronts.

First, the Church was hard at work on a "Design" which would give substance, shape and effective witness in the Christian mission. Second, the two Conventions were continuing their merger courtship. Third, the Black Manifesto and urban upheavals would give rise to General Assembly Resolution No. 19 and the Reconciliation Fund program. Fourth, the National Convocation of the Christian Church (Disciples of Christ) would supplant the NCMC. And fifth, a few days after the demise of the National Christian Missionary Convention in Lexington, Kentucky, a Black Disciples of Christ Caucus developed informally and became a stimulant for creative movement in those historic and pregnant times.

Indeed, between 1968 and 1971 the Christian Church (Disciples of Christ) gave birth to ecclesiastical quintuplets!

## CONVENTION MERGER

The Joint Committee on Merger had several task forces and full fifteen-member committee meetings to refine, "A Proposed Recommendation on Principles for the Merger of the National Christian Missionary Convention and the International Convention of Christian

Churches (Disciples of Christ)." The following are excerpts from that recommendation which was adopted by the Fifty-second Session of the National Christian Missionary Convention. The meeting took place at Jarvis Christian College, August 20-25, 1968:

1. That the National Christian Missionary Convention and the International Convention take enabling action at their 1968 meetings to provide for the merger of the National Christian Missionary Convention's business functions with the International Convention of Christian Churches (Disciples of Christ) or its successor...

2. That the National Christian Missionary Convention become the National Christian Church Conference which shall be directly related administratively to the International Convention of Christian Churches and shall meet for purposes of providing a forum for the discussion of pertinent issues related to Negro life in the context of the total church life; program promotion; leadership training; fellowship; and such other general purposes as shall support and strengthen the congregations involved in the total mission of the church...

3. That, with the mutual agreement of the National Christian Church Conference and the United Christian Missionary Society, the International Convention shall employ an Administrative Secretary ...whose responsibilities shall include:

a. Serving as Administrative Secretary of the National Christian Church Conference;

b. Bearing national administrative responsibility for developing consultations with states/areas (regions) to the end that state/area (region) structures, programs and services be effective to Negro congregations in each state/area (region)...

The main body of the recommendation was supplemented with suggestions on how it could be implemented. The Jarvis Christian College 1968 session of the National Convention accepted the recommendation "and that the committees indicated be empowered to implement." A companion action was taken by the International Convention during its September 1968 session in Kansas City, Missouri.

Kenneth L. Teegarden played a major role in drafting the new restructure principles for the Church. He was also assigned the task of aiding in the development of "Proposed Next Steps in Implementing the Merger of the National Christian Missionary Convention and the International Convention." A task force consisting of Raymond E. Brown, Emmett J. Dickson, and Kenneth A. Kuntz met with Teegarden to work out the details of these steps.

The NCMC Board of Trustees met in Hawkins, Texas, April 29-30, 1969, received the report of the drafting task force, and developed the following merger recommendations to be forwarded to the final meeting of the National Convention in Lexington, Kentucky, August 5-10, 1969:

1.  The name of the organization shall be the "National Convocation of the Christian Church (Disciples of Christ)."

2.  The General Office of the Christian Church (Disciples of Christ) should proceed with the necessary steps to name an Administrative Secretary with executive portfolio to carry responsibility for the National Convocation of the Christian Church.

3.  Whenever naming such an Administrative Secretary, the General Office shall consult with the Executive Committee of the National Christian Missionary Convention (or the National Convocation of the Christian Church (Disciples of Christ), and the administration of the United Christian Missionary Society.

4.  The establishment in the General Office of the position of Administrative Secretary for the Convocation should include an adequate job description that would include:

    (a)   Responsibility for developing the total life and witness of congregations, especially Negro congregations;

    (b)   Responsibilities for any program and services shall be coordinated through liaison relationships with the Division of Church Life and Work of the United Christian Missionary Society.

    (c)   Service as Administrative Secretary for the Committee on Interim Developments in Negro Church Life;

    (d)   Responsibility for the development of consultative processes leading to adequate and effective structures, programs and services to Negro congregations in all the regions; and administrative units of the church.

5.  Negotiations shall be conducted between the general office of the Christian Church and the United Christian Missionary Society regarding the funding of the new office of the Administrative Secretary, which may include possible transfer of funds to support this office, but programming for the Convocation and the School of Faith and Life should continue to be developed through regular program channels.

6.  Consultations should be continued to determine the future administrative focus and resources of the "Star Supporter" program in order to preserve its values and to increase its effectiveness.

7.  Specific legal procedures for continuing the legal integrity of the NCMC corporation have been developed with legal counsel.

8.  Specific proposals for the organization of the National Convocation have been approved by the NCMC Board of Trustees for submission to the NCMC Assembly, August 5-10, 1969. Upon approval of the Articles of Operation by the NCMC Assembly the NCMC Assembly should adjourn sine die (indefinitely), and the first meeting of the National Convocation be convened to elect officers under the Articles of Operation.

9.  The General Office of the Christian Church should proceed with implementation of the merger dealing with employment, appointments and elections.

In order to clarify the provision in the merger agreement that "the legal integrity and the purposes of the National Christian Missionary Convention, Disciples of Christ, Inc. be preserved," seven additional stipulations were added under item two in the original document. These stipulations dealt with money received from the sale of any property owned by the Convention; reformation of a Board of Trustees to reflect the mode of a National Convocation operation; duties and responsibilities of the corporation, its board and officers; and the distinctive role the National Christian Missionary Convention to have its trustees receive, hold, sell, lease or dispose of any real estate or personal property owned by the Convention.

These recommendations were brought to the 1969 session where they received a unanimous adoption. Raymond E. Brown, who was elected NCMC President had the distinction of being elected the last President of the Convention per se. He completed his two-year tenure by serving the second year as the first President of the National Convocation of the Christian Church. He had played a key role in drafting the final merger agreement and suggesting the guidelines for the formation of the National Convocation.

During the historic final session of the NCMC held on the campus of Transylvania University in Lexington, Kentucky, President Brown greeted those attending with these words:

We meet representing what may be called a predominantly Black Convention seeking to implement a merger with what may be called a predominantly White Convention. We meet at a time when it is unpopular for Black people to be anything short of proponents of separateness; when it is popular to create unrest; when tensions between peoples are mounting higher and higher; when there are those who want to be where the action is, and yet be true, faithful and just to the principles and heritage of those who established both the Church and the National Christian Missionary Convention; but more especially to Him whom we have committed our lives.

The president's greeting had aptly described the socio-religious conditions within which the final session of the NCMC convened.

## MERGER AND THE SOCIAL REVOLUTION

Both the Conventions and the congregations had been immersed for several years in a restructure and realignment struggle. Consummation of the merger of Conventions had come amidst the social upheaval and turmoil in the cities. Many church leaders—African-American and Anglo-American—saw a definite relationship between the successful merger of Conventions and meeting the crisis in the cities.

John R. Compton of Cincinnati/ Cleveland, Ohio, who had been seconded from the Ohio Christian Society staff to give administrative assistance for the Urban Emergency Action Program. He was selected to be the first Administrative Secretary of the National Convocation. Now African-American church interests and competent leadership presence was lodged symbolically in the heart of the Church—the General Office of the International Convention. The Executive worked alongside the General Minister and President and other General Office staff. Black executive staff leadership now had an opportunity to develop peer relationships with all general and regional staffs serving congregations.

No longer did the whole task of servicing African-American congregations fall on two or three overworked and underpaid staff persons. The entire professional field staff of the general and regional church were expected to service all of the Disciples of Christ congregations— including those who were pre-dominantly African-American. We were on the threshold of moving from 'Objects of' to 'Partners in' the mission! The whole Church was getting into a better position to deal effectively with the issues being raised by the burning cities.

## THE RECONCILIATION FUND IS BORN

The International Convention had been responding to the rising tide of the civil rights movement in a number of low-key but significant ways. Widespread debate was held in St. Louis, Missouri, October 13-18, 1967 during an Assembly debate on Resolution No. 62. The resolution dealt with a National Council report on civil disorder. On March 4-5, 1968, the Urban Emergency Action Committee of the Disciples of Christ was formed through the Division of Church Life and Work of the UCMS. Following study of National Council of Churches of Christ documents and studies of the issues, the UEA selected a "Steering Committee" to guide a program called "Reconciliation: The Urban Emergency Program of the Christian Church." Some thirty states and areas of the Christian Church (Disciples of Christ) contributed approximately $2 million from 1967 to 1969 in support of this program.

The struggle was sharpened by the development of THE BLACK MANIFESTO by H. Rap Brown and other militant Black leaders in 1967. The situation reached a climatic point with the assassination of Martin Luther King, Jr. on April 4, 1968 on the portico of the Lorraine Motel in Memphis, Tennessee. The assassination set off more than 100 incidents of civil disorder and caused the deaths of forty-three persons.

On May 27, 1969 the General Board of the International Convention, of Christian Churches meeting in St. Louis, was motivated by the course of secular events to "call upon the church to engage in actions that confirm our earnest pledge to bring forth God's grace and the fruits of repentance. We recognize both the magnitude of the actions we recommend and the painful readjustments in our corporate life they will require. We are sensitive to the major re-examination of all priorities in our church life that will be involved. However, we feel that repentance without pain is suspect, and these readjustments are small measured against the price in human hurt the abused among us have been forced to pay."

The General Board recognized the need to work for legislation and governmental action and problems of racism and poverty in both rural and urban areas. It then went on to recommend that "Reconciliation: The Urban Emergency Program of the Christian Church" be extended from two years to four and the goal be raised to $4 million of newly given monies.

Program agencies were challenged to deploy ten percent of their annual operating and capital funds for the first four years of the decade into programs dealing with the crisis. Local congregations were urged to consider deploying five percent in a similar manner. Administrative units were advised to use fifteen percent of their investment portfolios in a manner to provide loans and support programs serving the poor and powerless.

Furthermore, all General Units of the church were challenged to develop a multi-racial staff. The Board felt that "the level of staff members from minority groups should reach twenty percent by 1975". It felt that the twenty- percent goal for minority representation should be sought for all Disciples of Christ groups belonging to "ecumenical delegations, ecclesiastical commissions, and institutional boards..."

## THE SEATTLE ASSEMBLY & RESOLUTION No. 19

RESOLUTION NO. 19 was an omnibus action, which was passed by the General Assembly in the August 1969 session in Seattle, Washington, as the response of the Disciples of Christ to THE BLACK MANIFESTO. Floor debate was participated in vigorously by restless African-American Disciples of Christ ministers like T. Garrett Benjamin of Indianapolis, Indiana, and James Blair of Kansas City, Missouri, of the newly formed the Black Disciples of Christ Caucus. They challenged those assembled to think deeply about the issues, which were laid before them. Special concern was expressed for an empowered racial/ethnic ministry. The emphasis upon twenty percent representation of minorities on General, Regional and congregational staffs, as well as on ecumenical delegations and church commissions, had planted the seeds for what would eventually be seen as an "affirmative action" program of the Christian Church (Disciples of Christ).

## THE EMERGENCE OF THE BLACK DISCIPLES OF CHRIST CAUCUS

With James Blair as chairman, the Black Disciples of Christ Caucus met at Second Christian Church of Indianapolis, Indiana, one month following the Seattle General Assembly to explore "the future relationship between the (Black) Caucus and the Spanish community." Black caucus leaders felt that the actions taken in Seattle required "Red, Black, and Brown Disciples to unify."

One month later during the December 7-9, 1969, meeting of the Home and State Missions Council in St. Louis, Missouri, the Black Caucus met and developed the following proposal. They asked for:

1. A voice in the expenditure in the $4 million Reconciliation Fund proposed by the 1969 Seattle General Assembly, and;

2. $20,000 from the General Church to organize and implement Regional Conferences on program priorities and needs.

The Caucus also agreed to seek a meeting with General Minister and President, A. Dale Fiers, to consider the promotion of the Minority Conference and related matters. On January 23-24, 1970 during a Black Caucus meeting at Second Christian Church of Indianapolis, Indiana, plans were mutually agreed on for holding three Spanish-speaking and seven Black regional conferences.

John R. Compton, the Assistant to the General Minister and President, met with the Black Caucus during the May 5, 1970, meeting of the Home and State Missions Planning Council. He informed the group that the Administrative Committee of the General Board had assigned the implementation of the idea of the Minority Regional Conferences to the Office of the General Minister and President. The General Minister and President was directed to "find the $20,000 suggested to finance the conferences."

Raymond Brown, then Vice-moderator of the General Assembly and staff for the Board of Church Extension, was freed from his staff responsibilities to assist John Compton and a special committee in coordinating the conferences.

## THE CONVOCATION-RECONCILIATION CONNECTION

Mindful of the suggestions made by the Black Disciples Caucus, General Minister and President, A. Dale Fiers, called a small task group of Convention/Convocation representatives to Indianapolis, Indiana, to give advice and counsel on making Reconciliation a permanent thrust of the Disciples of Christ. Gerald Cunningham, a Black staff person in the Department of Church and Society in the UCMS Division of Church Life and Work, provided six months of administration as Director of "Special Congregational Services" as they related to Black congregations and Reconciliation. He was to be followed by John Compton of Cleveland / Cincinnati, Ohio, who was employed to serve full time as Administrator for Reconciliation.

The experience of the Steering Committee for Reconciliation was varied but limited. Now the General Assembly had given it a broad church-wide mandate to promote educational monitoring as well as a grant program. Prior to the Seattle Assembly, Convention President Richard L. Saunders of Brooklyn, New York, had urged Barton A. Hunter, the UCMS Executive responsible for the administration of the Urban Emergency Action Program, to look more favorably upon Black congregations already lodged in the central cities as a means for carrying out Reconciliation programs.

Citing a position paper distributed by the Board of Directors of the National Committee of Negro Churchmen, Saunders lifted up the following excerpt for Hunter:

The White religious establishment should take with utmost seriousness the Black church as the only, though imperfect, link with the inner city life for the mission of the church. We insist that the mission structure of the national denominations must identify with, and be led by the Black churches if their efforts are to have either credibility or reality... The Black church already has a physical presence in these communities. This presence and its organization is available as a means by which the whole Christian community can deal substantially and effectively with the urban crisis. (Letter to Barton Hunter, Indianapolis, Indiana, —from Richard Saunders, Brooklyn, New York, June 4, 1968)

The task group advising select chief administrators of agency units lifted up this strategy during the consultation. When the criteria for making Reconciliation grants was finally adopted, it was agreed that grants would be made to national or multi-regional programs which are related to African-American, Hispanic, or other minority congregations of the Christian Church (Disciples of Christ). They were required to meet one or more of the following:

1) Strike at the root causes of poverty and discrimination;

2) Seek to change unjust systems (e. g. laws, institutions, company practices);

3) Seek to overcome the injustices which racial minorities and the poor face;

4) Seek to achieve empowerment of groups with opportunities for self-development.

Policies were established that called for the membership of the steering committee to have a majority of minority members and the staff executive to be a member of a minority group.

## IMPLEMENTING THE CENTRAL CITY-CONGREGATION PRIORITY

Gerald Cunningham's short-term assignment in 1968 to provide special services to predominantly Black congregations as they related to Reconciliation initiated an abiding concern for the Division of Church Life and Work (now called the Division of Homeland Ministries). As a member of the UCMS Urban Emergency Action Staff Committee, Cunningham established a network of Church Action for a Safe and Just Community projects, which received a portion of operational funding from Reconciliation. These programs originated in approximately twenty-five to thirty Disciples of Christ racial/ethnic congregations throughout the country, impacting not only central city but also rural communities. Among these congregations were Grove Park Church, Kinston, North Carolina; La Harmosa Church, New York, New York; Macedonia Church, Birmingham, Alabama; Second Church, Hagerstown, Maryland; Free Grace Church of Christ, Plymouth, North Carolina; St. Marks Church, Mobile, Alabama; Segunda Christiana, Bronx, New York; Third Church, Warren, Ohio; Washington and Norfolk District Assembly, Roper, North Carolina; and First Church, Kansas City, Missouri.

CASJC sponsored a variety of community directed programs. These included prevention of negative youth behavior, voter registration, legal defense efforts for the powerless, preparation for employment and job awareness.

The attempt of the Division of Church Life and Work to serve a larger number of African-American congregations was strengthened February 15, 1971 when Enoch W. Henry, Jr., senior pastor of United Church in Los Angeles, California, began general staff employment as Director of Special Services in the Department of Evangelism and Membership in the newly named Division of Homeland Ministries. He was given a broader responsibility than Cunningham. According to Executive Chairman Kenneth Kuntz, he was "to give particular attention to congregational renewal and life-style that will have increased relevance and effectiveness in mission."

Reconciliation provided a portion of the operating cost for the new portfolio and Henry gave particular attention to aiding African-American congregations promoting these ministries. The coming of Enoch Henry to the General Staff helped to fill a void created in 1962 by the resignation of Charles H. Webb, Sr. and his acceptance of the call to pastor Park Manor Church in Chicago, Illinois. Within the first year Henry had established service relationships with thirty-one congregations in cooperation with fourteen Regional Church staffs. Some were predominantly African-American; others interracial, and one ecumenical.

Convocation-related congregations, which were located in the central cities where many social and human needs existed, were given priority consideration for Reconciliation grants. Among those congregations receiving grants were Hillside Church, Indianapolis, Indiana; West Paseo Boulevard Church, Kansas City, Missouri; United Church, Detroit, Michigan; First Christian, Saginaw, Michigan; Central Church, Kansas City, Missouri; United Church, Cincinnati, Ohio; United Church, Jackson, Mississippi; Quindaro Church, Kansas City, Kansas; Twelfth Street Church, Washington, D. C.; Mills Street Church, Oakland, California; Willow Street, Hannibal, Missouri; and Wildewood Church, Oklahoma City, Oklahoma.

John Compton was the administrative director of Reconciliation during its initial "emergency status." Thomas Griffin was assigned as the Staff Associate for Reconciliation Promotion. In 1970 when the National Convocation was born, Compton became an Assistant to the General Minister and President. His primary assignments were: (a) Administrative Secretary of the National Convocation, (b) convener of the Reconciliation Committee and (c) the Chairman of the Committee on Interim Developments in Negro Church Life.

On September 1, 1970, Thomas Griffin was appointed as Staff Director of Reconciliation and Compton, then Assistant to the General Minister and President, continued as convener of the Committee. This arrangement held true until 1972 when General Assembly Resolution No. 48 Concerning Reconciliation Beyond 1972 went into affect. A committee was elected by the General Board with at least seven of its members being from racial/ethnic groups. William K. Fox succeeded John Compton as an Assistant to the General Minister and President and served as Staff Director of Reconciliation. However, on June 1, 1977, when Thomas J. Griffin resigned as Director of Promotion to return to the pastorate. Ernest J. Newborn of Jefferson City, Missouri, was called May 1, 1978 to be the Administrative Director of Reconciliation. He became responsible for both the administration and promotion of the program.

The National Convocation Executive has always been the Chairman of the Reconciliation Committee. This has assured a Convocation connection as well as an official relationship to the Office of General Minister and President. The five ex-officio members of the Steering Committee were constituted by General Minister and President, A. Dale Fiers, (and his successor Kenneth L. Teegarden); Church Finance Council President Spencer Austin, and President of the Division of Homeland Ministries Kenneth A. Kuntz. The Director of Reconciliation and the Convocation Administrative Secretary rounded out the five ex-officio members.

Thus, the merger of convention agreement was more than a bureaucratic exercise in document development. Here are some specific goals that were met: (a) establishment of the Reconciliation Fund as a permanent thrust in the mission of the Christian Church (Disciples of Christ); (b) the adoption of General Assembly Resolution 19; (c) the launching of the National Convocation; and (d) eventual adoption of the Provisional Design for the Church. The Church was in a position to make creative and substantive responses to the crises in the cities, towns, and the world. The first two General Ministers and Presidents of the Church, A. Dale Fiers and Kenneth L. Teegarden, and General Unit Presidents Spencer Austin, and Kenneth A. Kuntz, were key factors in the maintenance of these important Convocation- Reconciliation relationships.

## CHAPTER THIRTEEN

# WORKING IN THE WHOLE CHURCH AND THE WHOLE WORLD: THE PARTNERSHIP BEGINS (1970 - 1975)

We begin with our feelings about the present state of the church and the nation. Within the church some gains have been made, and for these we are grateful. But there is much to be done. Leadership positions in White congregations are almost totally closed to Blacks.... It raises a serious question as to whether such congregations have any understanding of the community of faith. It is magnificently ironic that the Christian Church (Disciples of Christ) is a national sponsor of Project Equality, a program designed to encourage nondiscriminatory employment practices among church suppliers. Yet most of our congregations flagrantly violate fair employment practices every time they call a pastor.

Our curriculum is White and middle-class, our hymn books the same. We resent this... Our Black congregations worship in ill-equipped buildings; our Black clergy are under-trained and under-paid. This is not the result merely of inadequate stewardship, though we confess the need for Black churches to improve their giving. Rather, it is the result of a century of neglect by White church structures and White church leadership. That neglect continues today...

—The Preamble to General Assembly Resolution No. 47 "Concerning Church, Nation and Black Disciples", 1971.

The early 1970's were the years when African-American Disciples of Christ set their mission sails for the holy tasks as peer Christians in the whole church and the whole world. Acting within the institutional body of a Christian church, which was striving to be true to God's high calling, was a very new thing for most of the National Convocation leadership.    Many knew only the workings of the International Convention. Nineteen-seventy brought on the decade of the four lane ecclesiastical highway.   No longer was the discipleship journey to be a lonely walk along a single, winding gravel mission road. The venture of faith was successful because the church had faithful and fearless leadership guiding most of the field service agencies, and creative field staff and congregational leaders in the majority of the Church Regions.

Key roles were played by the following African-American Disciples of Christ leaders: Emmett J. Dickson, James Blair, Harvey Thomas, John R. Compton, Paul Sims, Raymond E. Brown, Elbie Titus, L. L. Dickerson, Rosa P. Welch, Carnella Jamison Barnes, A. C. Stone, Lorenzo J. Evans, Gerald Cunningham, T. Garrott Benjamin, Jr., and Robert L. Saunders.

But equally important, alongside the Convention/Convocation leaders were Anglo-American Disciples of Christ leaders like Gaines Cook, Thomas J. Liggett, A. Dale Fiers, Kenneth Kuntz, Spencer Austin, Kenneth L. Teegarden, Barton Hunter, Helen Spaulding, Rolland Sheafor, James Rainwater, and W. Elbart Starn.  They cast their lot with the prophetic emphases in the Christian gospel. Though often misinterpreted and misunderstood, these leaders provided a steadfast and persistent leadership for the Church in these most trying of times. This is only a partial roll call. There were many others—African-American and Anglo-American—with similar mind and commitment to human equality and social justice. The energies of the Black Disciples of Christ Caucus were soon absorbed into the first Board of Trustees of the National Convocation of the Christian Church (Disciples of Christ).

## THE NATIONAL CONVOCATION BEGINS TO LIVE

The first Biennial Assembly for the National Convocation of the Christian Church (Disciples of Christ) took place August 19-23, 1970, at Columbia College, Columbia, Missouri, with 232 representatives registered from seventeen states and the District of Columbia. John R. Compton, as an Assistant to the General Minister and President, served as Administrative Secretary for the Convocation. The rationale behind the selection of an all-Anglo-American Disciples of Christ-related woman's college was to make an intentional effort to expose both races to different cultural-religious settings. It would also acquaint them with one another as human beings and children of God.

Bringing an interpretation of what the merger of Conventions now meant for Black people in the Christian Church (Disciples of Christ) became a critical priority for the first Convocation Administrative Secretary and the Board of Trustees. The time of history and the prevailing attitudes on race relations in the United States, made the task of interpreting the merger extremely difficult.

John Compton was the Chairman of the Steering Committee for Reconciliation as well as Staff Director and the Administrative Secretary. Churches were in the midst of an extensive monitoring of the service agencies and congregations in relationship to their commitment and implementation of Resolution No. 19. An "Affirmative Action" questionnaire was developed by the Reconciliation Committee and Compton sent it to all congregations, General Units, Regional organizations and institutions. Dr. Compton was receiving, evaluating and summarizing the data in time for the General Minister and President to report to the General Board, meeting that October 1971, in Louisville, Kentucky.

## THE BACKGROUND FOR GENERAL ASSEMBLY RESOLUTION NO.47

Convocation leadership began with a determined effort to bring African- American Disciples of Christ church and community concerns up front and center in the life of the whole church. Partnership in the mission now required that the official church action of congregational representatives take place in the "main arena"—that is, the General Assembly.  This meant that the National Convocation functioning through out the year via a Board of Trustees and an Administrative Secretary, had to devise a way to promote three-way communication between the Convocation Office, Board of Trustees and the congregations to assure that all major wants and needs surfaced. Once surfaced, it was the responsibility of the Administrative Secretary and Board of Trustees to encourage and/or enable the Church to respond to those wants and/or needs.  Black Disciples of Christ found themselves in the "hard ball game of ecclesiastical bureaucracies." They had some experience in doing this but not with the "main arena." A tremendous challenge lay ahead.

Administrative Secretary Compton and the Board were anxious to try the new system for setting program priorities in the church. The Administrative Committee of the General Board had already directed the Office of the General Minister and President to "find" $20,000 to implement a series of "minority conferences" mainly for African-Americans and Hispanics. The Convocation Board of Trustees also asked for six Schools of Faith and Life to be held in Alabama, Texas, Mississippi, South Carolina and Virginia during the summer of 1971.

A compromise was reached whereby the "minority conferences" were planned and launched as proposed with some of the ingredients of a School of Faith and Life included. John Compton developed an African-American church priority setting process in connection with these conferences. In-put from the "minority conferences", consideration of data already available in the Dale Medaris YEAR BOOK study, Carrie Dee Hancock field study and the intensive "Design for Renewal and Growth Among Negroes" NCMC report, provided Dr. Compton and the Convocation board with the substance for "omnibus" resolutions. These two resolutions, No. 46 and 47, were placed before the Louisville, Kentucky, General Assembly October 16, 1971. There was also an intense awareness of the social climate in the U.S. and the world, which was making a substantial impact on the Christian mission.

## RESOLUTION NO. 46

Resolution No. 46, Concerning Establishment of a Committee on Black Church Work, was a vehicle for monitoring program services. It was intended to supplant the "Interim Committee on Developments in Negro Church Life." The new Committee was designed to give a panoramic view of the entire church life and work as it related to Black people and thus involve interaction with all program units and institutions serving the congregations. Further, the new Committee was to "have direct contact with the church cabinet, administrative committee and the General Board of the Christian Church (Disciples of Christ) through the Office of the General Minister and President."[1]

The purpose of the new Committee was to:

* hold in review the whole work of the Christian Church as related to the Black constituency and,

\* review, correlate and evaluate plans and programs of the various units as now envisioned for a more meaningful, significant and effective witness of the church.

The committee was to consist of up to twenty persons and be a part of the General Office. They would be appointed by the General Minister and President "after consultation with the appropriate executive." One representative each was to come from the Board of Church Extension, Board of Higher Education, Conference of State Secretaries and Board Chairmen, Unified Promotion, Division of Overseas Ministries, Reconciliation, Christian Board of Publication, and remainder from the Division of Homeland Ministries and the National Convocation—one of whom was to be the president of the National Convocation. The Convocation was to assure that there was a majority of Blacks on the Committee and the Administrative Secretary of the Convocation was to Chair the Committee. Twice a year a meeting would be held for two days with time allowed the evening before for "A Caucus of Black members "...to discuss plans and programs on the two-day agenda."

## BLACK CHURCH PROGRAM PRIORITIES

Resolution No. 47 provided the immediate agenda for the Committee on Black Church Work. The resolution was Concerning Church, Nation, and Black Disciples and dealt with specifics.[2] Following a six paragraph general appraisal of the church and world from the perspective of African-Americans as Christian citizens, the Convocation challenged the General Assembly to resolve:

1. That a minimum of five additional Black ministers per year be provided salary supplement...

2. That a minimum of eight new Black congregations be established within the quadrennium...

3. That the program materials, church literature, hymnals, etc. be developed either denominationally or ecumenically to be more relevant to the needs of Black people...

4. That some adequate means of communication (newsletter, tabloid) be designed and funded to inform Blacks about relevant issues that affect them...

5. That at least twenty Black Christian leaders/pastors per year during the quadrennium have the opportunity for continuing education experiences financed in part by the appropriate department; and that a major program of Black student recruitment for the ministry/

ministry-related professions be supported; that a Black staff person (preferably under 30) be assigned to coordinate and implement this program and that ample scholarship funds be made available to sustain these persons while in pursuit of their degrees...

6. That the Christian Church establish an emergency minority ministerial support fund for minority persons who graduate from seminary and cannot be placed because of their race or color...

7. That the appropriate Division be authorized to formulate plans to seek $1,000,000 in additional dollars for Jarvis Christian College's Endowment Fund...

8. That the General and Regional Units of the Christian Church begin January 15, 1972, to observe a holiday in honor of Martin Luther King, Jr. and work to obtain legislation declaring a national day of remembrance each year.

9. That support be given to ending American involvement in Vietnam by a fixed date. Blacks are bearing more than their share of the casualties in this senseless war...

10. That the Christian Church (Disciples of Christ) support a reordering of the national priorities with a reduction of military expenditures being matched by an increase in money for human needs in our own nation and around the world...

Be it further resolved that the Committee on Black Church Work be called upon to keep these as well as other concerns under constant review, and to evaluate and report on progress to the ...General Board and to the ...General Assembly of the Christian Church (Disciples of Christ)...

The resolution was adopted by the General Assembly. The resolution advised the Office of the General Minister and President to forward those aspects of the resolution to the program units who should logically be responsible for implementing the action. African-American Disciples of Christ were on their way in "working the system" to achieve churchly goals.

### THE IMPLEMENTATION OF RESOLUTION NO.19

During this historic Louisville, Kentucky, General Assembly John R. Compton, as an Assistant to the General Minister and President and Convener of the General Steering Committee for Reconciliation, provided General Minister A. Dale Fiers with a report on how the church was responding to Resolution No 19. The report noted that within the congregational manifestation of the church where "outreach is within reach," the message of Resolution No. 19 appeared to "be slow in getting action." Out of the 4,000 plus congregations in the Church, 707 returned the questionnaire. Only 201 or 28 percent of them had made any effort to respond to the challenge of Resolution No. 19. Nearly half of the respondents (323) had no political education program. And 409 or 57 percent had maintained the same level of response to Reconciliation ministries since the Resolution No. 19 challenges.[3]

The greatest evidence of response to the call to increase Reconciliation efforts was found in the General Units, institutions and Regional organizations of the church.

Nine of the sixteen General Units had actually spent $6,173,201 on programs they deemed to be of a Reconciliation nature. Another $1,817,540 had been spent in like manner by eleven of the Institutions. Out of the thirty-four Regional organizations who returned questionnaires, twenty-one had spent $466,133.20 on programs, which dealt with minority group needs.[4]

In addition to direct support of specific programs, these manifestations of church had invested in "institutions that engage in regular low cost loans to the poor, the powerless and the racially alienated, with special consideration for minority-controlled banks, savings and loans and businesses." Most of the General Units and approximately half of the institutions and Regional structures were making some progress in the employment of minorities and encouraging their involvement on the respective boards and committees.[5] The progress in doing Reconciliation ministries seemed too slow for some and much too fast for others. It appeared to many concerned church people that nothing since the days of slavery and the Civil War itself had quickened the social consciousness of the Christian Church (Disciples of Christ) more than Resolution No. 19.

## CHAPTER FOURTEEN

# WORKING ON THE ADOPTED AGENDA or THE CONVOCATION'S ROLE IN ENABLING THE REALIZATION OF BLACK CHURCH PRIORITIES (June 1972 to the Present)

The Black church person and the Black local church in a White structure must possess a number of traits to be active, effective and true to what God has done in the Black experience. He or she must be able to cope with the White establishment while at the same time maintain contact and emotional ties and involvement in the Black liberation struggle. A dual kind of existence is required of those who would be a part of White institutions and at the same time be responsive to the Black experience.
—*Gilbert Caldwell, New York Theological Seminary, 1976*

Even white ants confer before they scatter.
—*I SPEAK TO THE WIND by Kofi Asare Opoku, University of Ghana, Legon, Ghana*

Work on the Convocation agenda began with the preparation for, and passage of, 1971 General Assembly Resolutions No. 46 and No. 47. The year following the adoption of these far reaching proposals, John R. Compton, the Assistant to the General Minister and President who had engineered their adoption, resigned to return to congregational ministry in Cincinnati, Ohio. On June 1, 1972, William K. Fox was called from a pastorate at Summit Christian Church in Dayton, Ohio, to succeed John

Compton as the Administrative Secretary for the National Convocation and Assistant to the General Minister and President.

During the final phases of the orientation of John Compton's successor, William K. Fox, Sr. expressed concern over the expansive nature of the proposed responsibilities. When Fox asked A. Dale Fiers how much staff in addition to himself did the Convocation office have, the GMP responded: "All the staffs in the seventeen program units of church plus the Regional staffs are at your disposal!" Dale Fier's answer threw the new Convocation

executive designate off balance with no leverage for a rational and meaningful response.

Two months later, on August 23-27, 1972, the Second Biennial Session of the Convocation was held at Atlantic Christian College, Wilson, North Carolina. There were many detailed tasks undone and final commitments from program personnel to be completed. Raymond E. Brown of Indianapolis, Indiana, had been a strategic and constructive participant in the development of the principles of merger. He continued as the National Convocation President. He became an accessible resource and help to the new Administrative Secretary. Vice-President Edith Richardson of Dallas, Texas, coordinated a comprehensive program geared to the Bible based theme—"Do You Love Me? Feed My Sheep."

Meeting on another predominantly Anglo-American Disciples church-related college campus satisfied one Convocation objective. But there were two additional Convocation goals. Foremost was to celebrate the election of Walter D. Bingham of Louisville, Kentucky, as the first African-American Moderator of the General Assembly. His election was the first church-wide dramatization of a key Convention merger principle. Second, by meeting in Wilson, North Carolina, the Convocation was trying to encourage attendance and fellowship with the 35,000 to 40,000 African-American Disciples of Christ members in the six Eastern Seaboard assemblies.

Moderator Bingham was given a Convocation award following his address at the Convocation banquet. Bishop James Gardner of New York delivered a sermon. All of the bishops in the six assemblies were invited by General Minister and President A. Dale Fiers to a luncheon meeting. This was the last Convocation biennial assembly that Dale Fiers attended before he retired.

The church had maintained long-standing program service relationships with African-American Disciples of Christ in the established Eastern Seaboard assemblies. During the formative years of the Convocation, the Board of Trustees and the Administrative Secretary wanted to strengthen the interaction, and understanding of church work advanced by both the Convocation and the Eastern Seaboard assemblies.

## AGENDA PRIORITIES AFFIRMED

In light of various actions of the National Convention, the 1971 General Assembly Resolutions Nos. 46 and 47 and the temper of the times, the Administrative Secretary urged the Board of Trustees to consider the recommendation of the following action priorities to the Convocation Assembly:

1.  Sponsorship of a Black minister's retreat in 1973;

2.  Establishment of a Commission on International Affairs with special consideration for Third World relationships;

3.  Securing of funds to promote the collection and publication of historical materials on Black Disciples of Christ;

4.  Appointment of an advisory committee on the church-wide financial campaign to assure inclusion of Black church needs;

5.  Sponsorship of an inventory of Black involvement in the life of the church and made available to the church at large;

6.  Setting of Biennial Assembly meetings for the next four years with an emphasis on Black Theology and "The Legacy and Task of the Black Church in the USA and the World;"

7.  Amending the "Articles of Operation" for the Convocation and;

8.  Making special recognition of services rendered to the Convocation and the general church by A. Dale Fiers, John R. Compton, and Mrs. Walter Griffin, Assistant to the Convocation Administrative Secretary.

The Wilson, North Carolina, Biennial Session adopted these suggestions. The Convocation was officially on its way in a partnership approach for implementing some of the long-standing Black church objectives.

## HELP FROM A COOPERATIVE CHURCH PRESS

Few Disciples of Christ had a complete understanding of how the National Convocation would "help develop new soul and life which can bring redemption for themselves (Blacks) and the whole Christian Church." There was need for clear and frequent statements of clarification to be communicated to all parts of the Church.

THE CHRISTIAN, (the weekly publication for the Disciples of Christ at the time), carried an article on the Convocation on July 23, 1972, called "New Challenges to Blacks."[1] It promoted the August 23-27, 1972, biennial session held at Wilson, North Carolina. The last year that WORLD CALL was published, the editor, James L. Merrell, devoted the entire September 1973 issue to "Black Disciples: A Special Report." Some fourteen writers contributed research essays on all aspects of Black Disciples of Christ—including the formation of the National Convocation.[2]

In April 1973, the Administrative Secretary initiated a monthly publication called UP-DATE ON THE BLACK CHURCH. The action taken was in fulfillment of General Assembly Resolution No. 47 which called for "some adequate means of communication (newsletter, tabloid), be designed and funded to inform Blacks about relevant issues that affect them...". The Office of Communication in the General Office as well as the church publications lodged in St. Louis, Missouri, continued to cooperate with the National Convocation in providing relevant print material.

## UNDERSTANDING AND UTILIZING THE BLACK EXPERIENCE

The problem of identity remained a challenge for Convocation leaders and supporters. The quest to achieve racial integration and the biblical conception of true community had motivated those who affected the merger of the Conventions. But now African-American people were being urged to assert themselves. The Convocation itself, was to be a means for conserving those spiritual and ethical values proven to be durable and viable within the Black experience. But what were those values and how were they to be conserved and projected within a pre-dominantly Anglo-American church?

One African-American Disciples of Christ leader maintained that well-intentioned Anglo-American Christian Church members were "eating up Negroes live and whole" in a quest for racial integration.

Like many, he feared the end would not only be the loss of Black religious experience in the church but also the loss of being.

During the same period that the National Convocation was born, African-American staff within six denominations formed an organization called Joint Education Development (JED). Their task was to find ways for working together on African-American church education.

Addressing an early meeting of that group, Lorenzo J. Evans, director of Christian Education for the Disciples of Christ, made observations on the meaning of the African-American experience like the following:

The Black church has a specific mission in ... providing a meaningful and viable educational experience for a people who have had, and are still having, what is called the "Black experience". The experience of being rejected, alienated, suppressed and mistreated in so many subtle ways simply because they are Black. The educational agenda for the Black church for the 1970's should be to equip a people with such an experience to share their insights and meanings for the enrichment of the whole church...

...there has never been developed guidelines to do education from the Black perspective dealing with these injustices...[3]

By 1975, JED had sensitized most leaders in the National Convocation as well as those in the other five cooperating Churches, to the necessity of taking this into account as they worked on General Church program goals.

This new awareness and quest to return to the best in the legacy of African-American people, led the Convocation Board of Trustees to select the predominantly Black colleges of Atlanta University, Atlanta, Georgia, for the Third Biennial meeting in 1974 and Fisk University, Nashville, Tennessee, for the Fourth Session in 1976. The Program Committee members for both Biennial Sessions were: President Claude Walker and Vice President Patricia Clark (1972-1974); and President Samuel W. Hylton, Jr. and Vice President Elizabeth Ennix (1974-1976). Under their leadership the Convocation had four years of exposure to three of the world's top Black theologians. These theologians dealt with Black theology as it related to the people and the times.

The Atlanta Session provided the Convocation with an opportunity to collaborate with the Disciples' Council on Christian Unity in bringing the African theologian, Kofi Asare Opoku of the University of Ghana at Legon, to dialogue with the widely known U.S. Black theologian, James Cone of Union Seminary, New York City. George Beasley, President of the Council on Christian Unity at the time, had met Opoku during several World Council of Churches Conferences on Theology. Their presentations provided the substance of significant dialogue at Spelman College, Atlanta, Georgia, and later were published in the journal edited by the Council on Christian Unity.

The following Biennial Session was similarly resourced by C. Eric Lincoln of Fisk University, Nashville, Tennessee. Elimo Njau, a Christian artist from Nairobi, Kenya, had been scheduled for the Nashville Biennial Meeting, but could not attend because his father died in Tanzania.

The Second Biennial Session attracted upwards of 300 registrants with more than 500 persons attending. The Atlanta, Georgia, and Nashville, Tennessee, meetings reached 648 and 725 in registrations alone with more than 1,000 in attendance. Following the Atlanta experience, the Convocation Board of Trustees decided that college campus facilities were no longer adequate for Biennial Sessions. At the Fourth Biennial Session in Nashville, Tennessee, it was announced that the Fifth Biennial Meeting would be at the Convention Center of Little, Rock, Arkansas. From that point on the Convocation leaders were committed to holding the Biennial Meeting in hotel and/or convention center facilities. A major agenda for Convocation President Samuel W. Hylton, Jr. following the Atlanta experience was the securing of larger and more adequate facilities for Little Rock, Arkansas. During the Nashville, Tennessee, Session it was announced that the Fifth Biennial Meeting would be in the convention center/ hotel facilities.

It was also urgent that the Board of Trustees devote itself to a revision of the original draft of the "Articles of Operation." This was necessary in order to establish the number needed for balanced representation on the Board and a more discrete definition of some of the officer responsibilities. By 1978 and the Fifth Biennial Session, Provisional Operating Guidelines were in place which covered: (a) the nominating process; (b) term of office; (c) handling of business items; (d) emergency items; and (e) eligibility for officers.

From the very beginning of the Convocation, it was agreed that no longer would a single congregation host the national meeting. The Region in which the Session was held would be the official host. A guidance manual for the host committee, similar to that used by Steering Committees hosting the General Assembly, had been developed in time for the Nashville, Tennessee, session. All Christian Church (Disciples of Christ) congregations within the immediate area of a Convocation meeting place were expected to be represented on the steering committee that hosted the Convocation.

## RESOLUTION NO. 19 AND BROADER REPRESENTATION

The Convocation had wholeheartedly supported the goals sought in General Assembly Resolution No. 19. It was especially concerned about having more lay persons on committees, boards, and holding offices. The Convocation demonstrated this commitment in Atlanta, Georgia, when Oscar Haynes of Washington, D. C. became the first lay person elected to the presidency of the organization. The Haynes administration began in 1978 with the Little Rock, Arkansas Session.

During World War II, African-American Disciples of Christ established the tradition of electing a woman vice-president. The constitution and by-laws designated the vice-president as chair and coordinator of the annual (or biennial) program. The person holding this position could make a meaningful impact on the substance and character of program if they were so inclined. In 1982 the Convocation broke this precedent and elected Cynthia L. Hale as its youngest and first woman president.

The Convocation had a similar concern for youth and young adults. The merger of program and services and the eventual integration of the two Conventions, significantly affected the ongoing relationships General African-American Disciples of Christ staff had with youth and young adults. A small number of young people and lesser number of young adults filtered into the wider church scene. Reaching young people through camps and conferences was now largely a responsibility of leadership in the regions and the remaining Black Church substructures in the states and areas.

The Convocation was persistent in the encouragement of Regional and General program unit staffs to be earnest and creative in reaching these age-levels. The Division of Homeland Ministries redefined the responsibilities of staff in the Department of Christian Education in order to continue many of the services previously provided by National Convention staff. Robert Glover, the Executive for that Department, honored the commitment made to Black Disciples of Christ Convention leaders. On June 30, 1974 after thirty years of meritorious service as a National Director in Christian Education, Lorenzo J. Evans retired.

His successor, Effie Blair of Houston, Texas, continued with a redefined portfolio. The church-wide, ecumenical program being featured by the national Joint Education Development on "Education in Black Churches," was given high priority.

## FOCUS ON YOUTH

The Division of Homeland Ministries secured a Director of Services to Church Youth. The emphasis shifted to the training of youth leaders for activities in the congregation as well as in the larger arenas of the church. The Convocation made an effort to symbolize its interest in youth by supporting the work of a "Youth Steering Committee."

In the early 1970's under the leadership of Amelia and Charles Webb, Jr. of Chicago, Illinois, and under the guidance of Ellen Annalla, DHM's newly employed Director of Services to Youth, workshops for youth were held during Convocation sessions. They dealt with Black literature, art and creativity, exploring levels of consciousness, and music. During the Fifth, Sixth and Seventh Sessions, a "Convocation Youth Choir" was organized and performed in selected plenary periods.

A dramatic approach to youth by the Convocation was made in 1973-74 when youth were recruited for membership in a Black Disciples of Christ Caribbean Youth Choir Study. Encouraged by cooperation from T. Garrott Benjamin and leaders at Second (now Light of the World) Christian Church in Indianapolis, Indiana, the Convocation collaborated with the Department of Latin America, and the pastors of Convocation-related Disciples congregations in Dayton, Columbus and Cleveland, Ohio. They were successful in recruiting twenty-five young people and advisors to sponsor the project.

## DEVELOPING A STYLE OF OPERATION

During the first five years of administrative life and work of the Administrative Secretary and Board of Trustees, there was earnest effort made to develop a credible style of churchmanship. Nothing like the Convocation had ever existed before within the structures of the Christian Church (Disciples of Christ). The challenges were many. One was to fulfill the role of advocacy for the concerns of African-American people as a whole and the African-American church in particular, while at the same time functioning as a partner with others carrying out the accepted tasks of Christian mission.

Another challenge was to function as a credible partner with others in mission enablement. This included the development of creative thought and plans of action in keeping with the New Testament. Finally, there was the ongoing challenge for effective communication and interpretation for all with whom there was contact and interaction-African-American constituents; peer staff in the program units; and church people as a whole.

Joseph S. Saunders of Dayton, Ohio, the former newspaper editor-owner and free-lance writer. He became the first Black professional to join the staff of the Disciples' Office of Communication. Saunders wrote several articles interpreting the role and nature of the Convocation. In October 1976, he contributed a brief feature column for UPDATE called, "Footprints and Shadows".

Saunders gives a lay person's first impressions from attending a Biennial Session of the Convocation. He describes it as a:

great family reunion with brothers and sisters...a gigantic evangelistic meeting with preaching, singing, and teaching...a mid-summer vacation...

And then in summary Saunders wrote:

The National Convocation is not a thing, nor a place, nor is it an event. The National Convocation is an experience. It is a sense of the past, the present and the future- all come together to form an unforgettable interlude in Black history... It is the ghost of Black saints long departed. It is the spirit of Black saints now marching in. It is the hope of the yet-to-be saints of tomorrow.[4]

It was this latter definition of the Convocation which emphasized the historic legacy from the "saints," which motivated many of the actions of staff and Board of Trustee members during the early years.

The Administrative Secretary needed to continually define the several ways Convocation supporters could get into the action of church. Dr. Fox suggested that without being a member of any committee, commission, or board a member of the Christian Church (Disciples of Christ) could:

* Send human and/or financial resources where they could not go...;

* Give constructive advice to those persons who represented them on committees, commissions and boards;

* Encourage such representatives to report in person and have dialogue with the congregation or church groups where they were members;

* Engage the church group and/or official board in a study of recommendations to be presented to a Regional or General Assembly;

* Support the sending of delegates from the congregation to Regional Assemblies with instructions to express the mind of the congregation on selected matters;

* Be open and willing to become an active member of a committee, commission or board whenever appointed or elected...; and

* Encourage the congregation of which you are a member to put "flesh and bone" on official policies and programs proposed by the Church- both Regional and General.[5]

But the Biennial Session of the Convocation—while not a body, which functioned in the legislative style of a convention—was a place for consultation, inspiration, learning, and recommitment. As Opoku pointed out in verse: "Even white ants confer before they scatter". Following every Biennial Session of the Convocation, Black Disciples of Christ scattered to make a difference in the name of Jesus Christ and his Gospel in all parts of the church and the world.

## CHAPTER FIFTEEN

# PARTNERSHIP IN THE MISSION TO "THIS MINISTRY"

...We have been taught- often without adequate appreciation of our own social, political, economic, and religious realities, or with insufficient understanding of our capabilities and gifts- to see ourselves as others see us. The first step toward answering the question of who we are must come from an awareness of the frame of reference we are to locate within in order to know ourselves... But the point is that we cannot allow the determination of who we are to be placed into, or as the case may be, outside of ourselves and in the hands of others no matter who they are. The Delphian oracle long ago gave good advice. "Know thyself!"

All this boils down to the fact that we must be anchored to the Rock even while geared to the times! Both extremes must be carefully avoided in the interest of truth... Perhaps as good a note to end this part of our exploration as any other is to call all of us, Black and White, evangelical, fundamentalistic, "Bible believing", or whatever, to the Scripture found in Luke 4:18: "The Gospel Is Liberation!"
—"Factors in the Origin and Focus of the National Black Evangelical Association", by William Bentley, pp. 310-321 in BLACK THEOLOGY: A DOCUMENTARY HISTORY, by Gayraud S. Wilmore and James H. Cone, 1966-1979

The African-American minister and the preaching of the Gospel combine to become the central ingredient for a witnessing, growing and effective congregation. Convocation initiatives led

141

the church to underscore this reality in the passing of General Assembly Resolution No. 47 the 1971 Louisville, Kentucky, General Assembly. During the Second Biennial Session of the National Convocation a recommendation was passed urging the church to revive the sponsorship of retreats for Black ministers and to increase opportunities for continuing education. The responsibilities for such programs, however, were assigned to the Department of Ministry and Worship in the Division of Homeland Ministries. The Convocation's task was to exercise its role of advocacy as well as provide advice and counsel so that these important ideas got off paper into functioning program.

DHM's President, Kenneth Kuntz, believed that nothing in the way of expanded ministerial services for Blacks as suggested in Resolution No. 47 should take place until a Director of Black Ministry was secured. One of the difficulties in the search was to find what the resolution had designated age-wise. It asked for "...a Black staff person (preferably under 30)...".

Clarence L. Johnson Jr. of Greenwood, Mississippi, a recent graduate of Tougaloo, Mississippi, was the first choice of the Division's search committee. He had an impressive collegiate record and was scheduled to enroll at Christian Theological Seminary, Indianapolis, Indiana. Early in 1971, agreement was reached on a plan for Johnson to enter CTS, be employed on a part-time basis by DHM, and initiate a research project on the status of the Black Disciples of Christ ministry. The study would not only satisfy one of the prerequisites for a Divinity degree, but also provide a fresh orientation to the service needs which might be included in a Director of Black ministry program.

On April 1, 1972, the arrangement was officially launched. A study of salary trends among African-American Disciples of Christ was underway by August 1972. Two-thirds of the 105 respondents reported receiving less than $5000 per year from congregations they were serving. That year Pension Fund studies showed the average annual compensation, including parsonage or parsonage allowance, for all Christian ministers to be $8,405. Fewer than a third of the respondents received any of the traditional "fringe benefits" provided for a full-time pastor. As a consequence, 59 percent of the respondents had other jobs in addition to serving one or more congregations. However, 90 percent indicated they were willing to serve one congregation full-time if an adequate salary was assured.[1]

The study convinced the Department of Ministry and Worship that special service needs for many African-American ministers existed. A job description was developed in line with Resolution No. 47 and the newly discovered needs. The full program was launched July 1, 1973 with Clarence Johnson becoming the first Director. Two Black pastors received ministerial support packages—one in Mississippi and one in North Carolina. Scholarship support was increased 50 percent for students preparing for ministry. Extensive financial support was given to a continuing education program on the campus of Atlantic Christian College, Wilson, North Carolina. It was pointed mainly toward the ministers in the Eastern Seaboard assemblies.

Finally, in August 1975, a National Retreat for Black Disciples of Christ became a reality. It was held in Indianapolis with more than 100 ministers in attendance. This annual event has attracted major church leaders and pastors from within and outside the denomination. It has been held in every section of the nation. Ministers serving every type and size of congregation consider this event an annual mainline renewal experience.

## RECRUITMENT AND SUPPORT OF MINISTERIAL STUDENTS

The Convocation maintained an interest in accelerating and improving the recruitment and financial support of ministerial students. The annual meeting of the National Christian Missionary Convention had been an occasion when most of the Star Supporter Fund money was received. Convocation groups like the Minister's Fellowship, Christian Men's Fellowship, and the Ministers' Wives Fellowship tried to give year-round promotion for the offering. From $6,500 to $10,000 had been realized annually through the Convention assembly.

When the Conventions merged and the convocation was formed it called for a Biennial Session to be held rather than an annual assembly. This meant that extra effort had to be put forth if giving to the Star Support Scholarship Fund was to be maintained.

Through the forceful leadership of minister's wives like Lucille Compton of Cincinnati, Ohio; Zola Walker of Hawkins, Texas; Edna Brown, Ruth Range, and guidance of veterans Reubena Fox, Zellie Peoples and Philandria Dickerson of Indianapolis, Indiana, the Ministers' Wives Fellowship devised "rules and procedures." They created a three-fold objective which included the raising of "money in our local congregations" to "compete in the contest which is designed for a church-related scholarship." Most of that money has gone to the Star Supporter Fund. Under the presidencies of Compton and Walker, a goal of $10,000 plus was first realized. A. C. Stone of Cincinnati, Ohio and Booker T. Dickson of Kansas City, Kansas/Washington, D.C., provided the stimulus for lay people and ministers to support the Star Supporter Scholarship Fund.

## THE DEPARTMENT OF CHURCH MEN

One of the benefits from the merger of the Conventions was the enhanced relationships developed between the various program units. One example is the collaborative relationship developed between the National Convocation and the Star Supporter Fund. Under the leadership of Elby Boosinger, then the Executive Secretary for the Division of Homeland Ministries Department of Church Men, Disciples of Christ laymen throughout the Church were encouraged to make financial contributions to the Star Supporter Fund. This promotion was highlighted during Christian Men's Fellowship retreats as a way to pick up the lag in giving to the scholarship fund in the odd-numbered years when the Convocation did not have a session.

From 1971 to 1979, a total of $83,787.46 was raised for the Star Supporter Fund. Of that amount, $43,787.46 came through the Department of Church Men. In 1980 an additional $9,788.27 was received in this manner for the Star Supporter Scholarship Fund. Note Table 3 which shows how 223 scholarship grants, or $315,260, was distributed from 1976 through 1987. A basic Convention/Convocation concern which once had been primarily the responsibility of the predominantly Black congregations, had now become a church-wide concern and opportunity for sharing with a variety of congregations and individuals.

During Convocation Biennial Sessions it became a practice for the Christian Men's Fellowship to lift up those receiving Star Supporter Scholarships. This was often done during a meal event sponsored by the Convocation's CMF constituency group. A glance at Table 4 shows the deployment of forty-five seminary graduates and recipients of Star Supporter Funds from 1976 to 1987. There is almost an equal number of persons who received Star Supporter Scholarships but did not graduate during this period. However, many of them have gone on to provide meaningful ministerial and/or humanitarian service.

## SCHOLARSHIP ADMINISTRATION

The Division of Homeland Ministries continued to administer all scholarship funds through Executive Secretary Thomas E. Wood and the Department of Ministry and Worship. The Convocation shared in the partnership through its members on the division's scholarship committee.

In 1974 a modest recruitment program was instituted through the Director of Black Ministry called the Person-to-Person Interpretation Program (PPIP). College and ministerial students in preparation for the Christian ministry were used in the summer to interpret ministry to high school students. PPIP continued on a low-key basis throughout the late 1970's with minimal success.

The National Convocation looked to the Office of Black Ministry for most direct as well as collaborative services. January 31, 1977 Clarence Johnson resigned as Director of Black Ministry to become the pastor of United Christian Church, Jackson, Mississippi. Ozark Range, Sr. of Columbus, Ohio, a minister with several years of pastoral and administrative experience in congregations and church institutions, succeeded Johnson on July 1, 1977. A mutually supportive relationship was developed between this office and the National Convocation.

## THE DIVISION OF HIGHER EDUCATION

The Division of Higher Education Board under the leadership of President William Miller inaugurated the Short Term Employment Experience in Ministry (STEEM) program in response to the 1969 Seattle, Washington, General Assembly Resolution No. 30. This resolution urged the Church to make special efforts to recruit Blacks and Hispanics for Christian ministry. STEEM was designed to provide experiences which suggested the options of Christian vocation to a college student. It was never intended to be a recruitment effort in a traditional sense.

However, DHE's interest in the maintenance of the STEEM program heightened after some initial successes and the passage of subsequent Resolutions like Nos. 46 and 47. These resolutions substantiated the wisdom of STEEM.

Annually, since 1971 from seven to ten racial/ethnic students have been placed in church-related employment situations. During the first ten years of operation, STEEM placed sixty-five college students in summer time short-term employment. Sixteen of those students chose Christian ministry as their calling. Several of the others went into people-helping professions. During the late 1980's, under the encouragement of DHE President D. Duane Cummins and NCCC Administrative Secretary John R. Foulkes, serious conversations on improved recruitment practices were initiated between the Board and the Committee on Racial/Ethnic Inclusiveness and Empowerment (formerly the Black and Hispanic Concerns Committee).

## CHAPTER SIXTEEN

# PARTNERSHIP IN MISSION TO CONGREGATIONS

Within the whole family of God on earth, the church appears wherever believers in Jesus Christ are gathered in his name. Transcending all barriers within the human family such as race and culture, the church manifests itself in ordered communities of discipline bound together for worship, for fellowship and for service, and in varied structures for mission, witness and mutual discipline, and for nurture and renewal of its members...

—*The Preamble of THE DESIGN FOR THE CHRISTIAN CHURCH (Disciples of Christ)*

A cue on strategy for reaching out to congregations was given to the Board of Trustees of the Convocation April 14, 1972. Minutes of a National Christian Missionary Convention committee charged to bring advice on the management of the Greenwood properties in Nashville, Tennessee. The committee constituted by Claude Walker, S.S. Myers, Kenneth A. Kuntz, Raymond E. Brown, and John R. Compton had suggested that the Convocation Board of Trustees utilize the framework of the Convocation Board, and the Committee on Black Church Work to support the Administrative Secretary in the development of "a plan and strategy for the future development and strengthening of the Black church".

Needless to say, the substance of that strategy had been developed several times in the past decade by African-American Disciple leadership. Beginning with the Seattle, Washington, General Assembly in 1969, omnibus resolutions relative to these concerns had been passed. It now remained the task of Convocation President Claude Walker to appoint a task force to reassemble this information in short form and propose priorities and a plan of attack for the remainder of the 1970's. President Walker included himself and the following persons to sit on this task force: T. Garrott Benjamin, Jr., Senior Minister at Second Christian Church (now Light of the World), Indianapolis, Indiana; Edna Ritchie, Associate Minister, Community Christian Church, Fort Worth, Texas; George Kearse, lay leader Stuyvesant Heights Christian Church, Brooklyn, New York; and Samuel W. Hylton, Jr., Senior Minister at Centennial Christian Church, St. Louis, Missouri.

The group met and, following extended sessions, they proposed the following "first level" and "second level" goals as priorities to be realized by 1979:

1.  Recruitment and leadership development;

2.  Established church development;

3.  New Church development; and

4.  Expansion through evangelism (It was understood that the Administrative Secretary would follow through on the need for better communication).

The following "second level priority goals" were proposed:

1.  Deputy system in program interpretation and development;

2.  Black Disciples of Christ historical materials;

3.  Specialized approaches to Pension Fund memberships; and

4.  Empowerment of the National Committee on Black Church Work.

The task force expressed anxiety about the sluggish pace with which African-American seminarians received placement in service following graduation. This was a particular concern for the pastor and membership of Second Christian Church, Indianapolis, Indiana. They had at least two members who were about to complete their seminary work with little or no promise of employment in sight.

There were at least twelve known vacancies in predominantly Black congregations. There were many others in predominantly Anglo-American congregations where seldom, if ever, attempts were made to contact prospective African-American candidates. The

Administrative Secretary was advised to launch an "emergency strategy for recruitment and placement."

The task force suggested the deployment of committee members and selected program staff to draft the detailed plans of action to realize the "first level goals." During the December 9-10, 1974, Convocation Board of Trustees meeting, the final report of the task force was considered. It was agreed that the following subjects merited consideration as possibilities for presentation to the 1975 San Antonio, Texas, General Assembly as resolutions:

1.  Field education and placement;

2.  New church establishment;

3.  Strengthening existing churches;

4.  Funds for UPDATE;

5.  Consultation on Church Union; and

6.  Relationships to Third World peoples.

The Convocation President, Samuel W. Hylton, Jr., picked up the leadership baton that was passed on by retiring President Claude Walker. The Convocation Board of Trustees and Administrative Secretary had never fully confronted the task of walking an idea through the institutional system to the point where it became an official resolution to be placed before the General Board and General Assembly. The walk included the following steps:

1.  Consultation with related program personnel and administrative units;

2.  Passing on suggestions to the Committee on Black Church Work for their evaluation, acceptance, and assignment to staff or appropriate program unit for refinement;

3.  Have the Committee on Black Church Work bring the "recommendation" to the Administrative Committee of the General Board through the proper Reference and Counsel group of the board;

4.  Allow the Administrative Committee to approve, disapprove, or recommend to the General Board for processing, or referral to the appropriate church program units for purposes of further refinement and action;

5.  And finally, if adopted by the General Board, the resolution becomes the "property" of the General Board. At that point it goes to the General Assembly where it can be debated, and then voted up or down.

This was the long path that the Convocation Board of Trustees and Administrative Secretary had to take on the "priority goals" if they were to be adopted by the General Church.

## NEW CHURCH ESTABLISHMENT BECOMES TOP PRIORITY

Following more discussion during the 1975 meeting of the Committee on Black Church Work, the proposal on new congregational establishment received top listing. General Minister and President Kenneth Teegarden joined the Convocation in expressing keen interest in this priority. Board of Trustee leaders originally pressed mainly for the establishment of new predominantly African-American congregations.

It was agreed that DHM's Executive Secretary of Evangelism and Membership, Loyal Northcott, would coordinate an inter-unit program staff task force to work on the details of a resolution for the San Antonio, Texas, General Assembly. Enoch W. Henry, Jr., Director of Special Congregational Services in that Department, was one of the staff serving on that task force. He was joined by program staff persons from the Board of Church Extension, Division of Overseas Ministries, Church Finance Council, and representation from the Conference of Regional Ministers and Board Chair persons.

Following an intensive examination of the financial and programmatic implications of such a resolution, a consensus was achieved on strategy. A draft of the resolution to be submitted would be sent to the Office of the General Minister and President for implementation through the Committee on Black Church Work and the Administrative Committee of the General Board.

Essentially, Resolution No. 69 on New Church Establishment called for the General Minister and President to become the catalyst for consultations with appropriate units and denominational leaders to work on the manifold aspects of such a major church-wide effort. Some of the urgency manifested by Black leaders for the establishment of new predominantly African-American congregations was lessened by this approach. However, it was established that 30 percent of all new congregation starts were to be predominantly African-American, Hispanic or Asian-American.

During the next six years, church-wide consultations were held. A new congregation establishment committee, under the chairmanship of Raymond E. Brown of the Board of Church Extension became operative. Racial/ethnic structures like the Convocation, Hispanic juntas, and Asian-American caucuses were involved in all deliberations and decisions. An informational program called "Church Advance Now (CAN)" was launched and the new Church-wide effort began.

At the close of 1986, CAN Program Director James Powell reported: (a) eighty-six new congregations established; (b) nineteen pastor/ developers recruited and trained; (c) thirty-two regions functioning with committees responsible for new congregation establishment; (d) eighteen regions had either completed or were in the midst of launching formal campaigns totaling $8.1 million in money for new congregation establishment! Supplemental program grants coming through the Board of Church Extension and the Division of Homeland Ministries totaled $175,450. Most (eighty-one percent) had gone to African-American and Hispanic projects. Eighteen percent of the new congregations established had been African-American, Hispanic or Asian-American— twelve percent short of the thirty percent goal!

Nevertheless, an idea born and a concept initially developed in the minds of Convocation leadership had been placed in the broad legislative stream of the church. The patient and courageous faith of many, had co-mingled with others in the church and at last were beginning to bear fruit for the kingdom.

The Convocation did not relinquish its concern for nurturing and empowering established congregations. June 30, 1974, Emmett J. Dickson, a pioneer in a variety of ways for thirty-eight years, retired. He had been the first and only Executive of the National Christian Missionary Convention; had served congregations in Texas; had been on the faculty at Jarvis Christian College in Hawkins, Texas; and was retiring from the Division of Homeland Ministries as Director of Field Services in the Department of Evangelism and Membership. Through a close association with the President of the Division of Homeland Ministries, various affiliated program staffs, as well as several Regional Church staffs, the National Convocation was able to encourage the provision of many services to established congregations. This reality was especially dramatized in the sponsorship of the Biennial Session program.

## THE SCHOOL OF FAITH AND LIFE

It has been previously noted how under the leadership of Patrick H. Moss, Vance Smith, Robert H. Peoples, and Lorenzo Evans the "institute" approach to Christian education was the major way to assist congregations. This activity continued through the era of the National Convention. One of the major commitments to Black Disciples of Christ in the merger of the Conventions was the agreement of the Division of Homeland Ministries to provide staff services for all School of Faith and Life-type events which occurred during the Biennial Session and/or other specified times.

The typical thrust and content of Convocation Schools of Faith and Life is found in the program for the Sixth Biennial Session, held in Cincinnati, Ohio. The program was directed by Effie M. Blair, who at the time was DHM's Director of Education for Minority Constituencies in the Department of Christian Education. Fourteen seminars which included the following topics were held: How to Get and Keep a Youth Group Alive; Saying YES to Faithful Stewardship; Family Life Styles: "Challenges and Choices; Methodologies in Congregational Growth;" "The Church Participating in God's Action in Community;" Creating Christian Education from Scratch; Making Your Older Years the Best Years; and Are You a Board or Bored Youth Leader?

Youth were encouraged to attend any of the seminars. However, a seminar entitled "For Times Like These" was for youth only. Its purpose was, "To explore options and look at role models in peer relationships, school, church and community". Effort was also made, "To discover how one's life is affected by: unemployment, career/ choice/planning, spiritual growth/Bible study, cultism, music and the Black experience.@ All seminars had the sharing of the latest materials available on the subject at hand. Participants shared ideas and experiences. Help was given on ways to deal with specific problems confronting the local congregation.

"Education for Congregational Empowerment" was the emphasis of workshops held in St. Louis, Missouri, during the Ninth Biennial Session of the National Convocation, August 5-8, 1986. The educational phase was under the leadership of Belva Brown Jordan, who had just been called as Director of Racial/Ethnic Educational Ministries in DHM's Department of Christian Education.

There were nine continuous workshops held for two hours per day for three consecutive days. In addition, ten personal growth workshops were conducted for two hours each and repeated daily. Subjects for some of the continuous six-hour workshops were: Empowering People to Lead; Evangelism in the Black Context; Eldership and the Diaconate; Understanding the Church's Mission; Strengthening the Black Family; Church Administration; and How to Start a Service Program in Your Church.

Personal Growth Workshops dealt with subjects like: Strengthening Prayer Life through the Bible as a Resource; Politics and the Black Church; and The Black Church in the year 2,000. Staff from the Division of Homeland Ministries and other church program units like the Church Finance Council, researched all of the workshops.

The School of Faith and Life concept has been adopted by most of the predominantly African-American Church substructures among Disciples of Christ in the east, southeast, south, and southwest. Regional and General Church staff participation in these events has been a major way to deliver field services to predominantly African-American congregations.

## CONTRIBUTIONS OF THE BOARD OF CHURCH EXTENSION: CONCERN FOR ESTABLISHED CONGREGATIONS

Historically, major program commitments for field services to congregations related to the National Convention/Convocation were first developed with the Board of Negro Evangelization/Christian Woman's Board of Missions/United Christian Missionary Society/ Division of Homeland Ministries- in that order. We have already referred to other agreements which were developed between units (e.g. Christian Board of Publication relative to the printing of a news publication).

However, in the late 1960's and early 1970's the Board of Church Extension, in the normal course of operations, became a major deliverer of services for the strengthening of established Convention/ Convocation related congregations.

In the mid-1960's the Board functioned as an "investment broker" for National Convention funds. Certificates of deposits were managed which produced earnings for the general day-to-day operations of the National Convention/Convocation offices as well as the Star Supporter Scholarship Fund. It has already been noted that it was a principal constructive respondent to the calls for affirmative action during the late 1960's and the passage of Resolution No. 19. The only General

Church unit to match the $75,000 advance to establish the Urban Emergency Program of 1968 was the Board of Church Extension.

Effective BCE staff leadership enabled BCE to make a real difference. First, was the administrations of three Board of Church Extension Presidents—William T. Pearcy, Rolland H. Sheafor and Harold R. Watkins. Each had differing management styles, but similar Christian conviction. They supported the development of basic policies and action developed which strengthened the established Convention/ Convocation-related congregation. And second was the employment of Raymond E. Brown of Hannibal, Missouri, in 1969 as the first Black professional general field representative. For several years he had been a successful pastor as well as the Secretary of the National Christian Missionary Convention.

Underlying the Board of Church Extension's approach to Convention/ Convocation related congregations was: (a) the intentional effort made to have African-American membership on its Board of Directors; (b) employ and up-grade professional Black staff; and (c) the liberalization of its loan and service policies—especially for predominantly Black congregations with under 200 members.

In the March 1974 issue of THE DISCIPLE (the bi-weekly Disciples of Christ journal), an article by Raymond E. Brown entitled: "Black Congregations: Four Years Have Made a Difference", was published. Prior to that time less than twenty-five percent of the National Convention-related congregations approached the Board for loans and other services. But after the period of 1970 to 1974, Brown was reporting "ninety-five different congregations..." requesting services. This meant that "almost (twice) as many as requested services in the prior ten years. And "even more significant," writes Brown, "are the 207 additional visits which represent services other than the initial general consultation."[1] These additional services, in addition to actual loans, included: architectural counsel; general planning and program assessment; fund raising, budget building and money management. Many of these services were offered free to congregations with limited budgets and under 200 members.

After these first four years there were "loans to seventy Black congregations totaling $3,112,566, of which $1,249,082 were interest free to thirty-nine congregations. Ten loans helped congregations purchase facilities for the first time. Fifteen loans provided new buildings, either the first for a congregation or rebuilding on the same site. Fifteen loans made it possible for congregations to relocate... Four congregations added educational space... Three bought adjacent properties... Two purchased sites for relocation and one purchased a parsonage."[2] All this occurred after intentional effort was made by the Board of Church Extension.

By September 30, 1987, twelve years later, Raymond Brown had become the Senior Vice President. In addition to the ninety-five congregations served during the first four years (i. e. 1970-1974), there were 146 that had been serviced. With understandable pride, Brown was able to pen the following summation: If new and improved facilities are a measure of the Church, then it is alive and doing well. Particularly is this true as it relates to the services which the BCE continues to provide Black congregations of the Christian Church (Disciples of Christ). Since 1970, as a result of good counseling, both as relates to finance and building, the following has been made possible:

61   congregations have new buildings including 11 new congregations;

96   have remodeled facilities;

44   added education and fellowship space;

12   purchased a parsonage;

13   purchased additional property; and

9    purchased new equipment.

The total loans to these congregations was $14,062,807, of which $2,178,202 was interest-free.[3]

## CONVOCATION RELATIONS WITH OTHER CHURCH UNITS SERVING ESTABLISHED CONGREGATIONS

Reference has been made to the Christian Board of Publication relationship with the Convention/Convocation to produce a news publication. Later, as will be mentioned in greater detail, there was collaboration with the National Convocation in the publication of historical materials. Equally important were the major Christian books and literature exhibits, with appropriate sales personnel, provided at every Convocation Biennial Session. The Board's biennial exhibit was a major resource for many of the church leaders in the smaller Convocation related town and country congregations.

Important alignments were made, both as Convention, and later as Convocation, with Unified Promotion/Church Finance Council to improve the performance of Christian stewardship in Convention/ Convocation established congregations. With the advent of the National Convocation and the employment of Thomas E. Griffin by the Church Finance Council, promotion for both Reconciliation and general Christian stewardship was launched. Special promotional materials were beamed toward Convocation related congregations.

An early piece of literature issued in March 1973 was called GET UNDERSTANDING. Featuring a likeness of the first African-American General Assembly Moderator, Walter Bingham, the one-sheet flier dealt with what "your money supports" and "How can you and your congregation participate?"

Later, in the late 1970's and early 1980's were tracts dealing with AWHAT'S HAPPENING?@ and ATHIS IS HAPPENING.@ Both pieces endeavored to point to the involvement of African-American Disciples of Christ in the total life and work of the church. They stressed the urgency for continued financial support if such involvement was to remain effective.

Another unit that worked with the office of the National Convocation in strengthening established church was the Pension Fund of the Christian Church (Disciples of Christ). Several conversations were held among the leadership on ways to increase the membership of African-American ministers in the Fund. Almost monthly, the Administrative Secretary of the Convocation was called upon by the Pension Fund to affirm the physical survival needs of a minister or minister's family and condone the provision of assistance from the Ministers' Benevolence Fund. Consequently, the Convention and Convocation leadership put forth special effort during the national session to promote giving to the Pension Fund's benevolence appeal. Too many of the Convention's / Convocation's own ministers and/or families had to call upon the fund for assistance.

## CHAPTER SEVENTEEN

# PARTNERSHIP IN THE MISSION FOR JUSTICE AND EQUALITY

Take away from me the noise of your songs, And to the melody of your lyres I will not listen. But let justice roll down like waters, and righteousness like a perennial stream.
—*(Amos 5:23-24)*

The Spirit of the Lord is upon me, because he hath anointed me to preach the gospel to the poor; he hath sent me to heal the brokenhearted, to preach deliverance to the captives, and recovering of sight to the blind, to set at liberty them that are bruised, to preach the acceptable year of the Lord.
—*(Luke 4:18-19)*

The Church of the "Open Door" with emphasis on racial and cultural inclusiveness requires evangelization and participation of Black people.
—*A Statement of Purpose: YEAST FOR THE LOAF—The National Convocation of the Christian Church (Disciples of Christ), 1973, Convocation Initiated Activity*

The Convocation has used both the unilateral and cooperative approaches in the Christian mission to achieve justice and equality for all people. Those actions which have been Convocation initiated have usually been through Board of Trustee motions carried out by the Administrative Secretary and an appropriate Trustee Board task force or committee. Often these actions were highlighted during the Biennial Session.

One notable action was the establishment of a "Liberation Award" in 1980 "for opening doors of service and empowerment for African-Americans and other oppressed peoples". The first recipients were William T. Gibble (National Benevolent Association), St. Louis, Missouri; Sandre R. Gourdet, Division of Overseas Ministries, Bolenge, Zaire, Africa; Kenneth A. Kuntz (Division of Homeland Ministries), Indianapolis, Indiana; Joe McClure (Greenwood Cemetery), Nashville, Tennessee; and Earl W. Rand (Jarvis Christian College), Hawkins, Texas. Among the subsequent recipients have been Kenneth L. Teegarden (Office of the General Minister and President) and Emmett J. Dickson (Division of Homeland Ministries and National Christian Missionary Convention).

Such recognitions had a relationship to the monitoring and advocacy function the Administrative Secretary and Convocation representatives carried on through involvement in the Committee on Black Church Work and the Steering Committee for Reconciliation.

Another Convocation initiated-type action was the purchase of a "Life Membership" in the National Association for the Advancement of Colored People in 1976. The Executive Secretary, Benjamin Hooks, was a principal speaker during the 1978 Little Rock, Arkansas, Biennial Session. The Convocation had representation in New York soon after to join African-American church persons in a show of solidarity on civil rights issues.

A little known function of the office of the Convocation occurs when the Administrative Secretary serves in a catalyst role for the periodic coming together of racial/ethnic General Church staff to share concerns. During the sharing of joys and heartaches as peers in the Christian ministry, justice and equality issues have arisen. A community of support has evolved. Careful examination of any justice or equality issue has sometimes required a show of solidarity and mutual desire to bring about reconciliation and/or rectification.

Staff members have been led to understand the interrelatedness of their directorships and field services. They get to know and understand more about the goals and purposes of peer staff—especially those in related program units. Team approaches to the provision of services to the field is encouraged.

## COOPERATIVE APPROACHES

Most efforts made toward the achievement of the justice and equality mission were done in partnership with others. This was particularly so within the institutional church. The system provided for the Convocation executive staff to chair the Reconciliation and Black Church (i. e. later Black and Hispanic) Committees. General Board actions in the mid-1970'S gave the Reconciliation Committee monitoring responsibilities and strengthened the Director's "ombudsmen's" status.

Functioning in this capacity, the Convocation, through its administrator, updated progress which was being made on Resolution No. 19. The Administrative Secretary reported the findings to the General Board for review in 1975.

An irregular and sluggish picture surfaced from the review and in June 1976 the General Board was prompted to order an in-depth evaluation of racial/ethnic employment practices by the Christian Church (Disciples of Christ). It charged "the General Reconciliation Committee to initiate separate meetings with the General Cabinet, Conference of Regional Ministers and Educational Institutions in the Board of Higher Education; to review the status of racial minority employment... to share specific plans that have succeeded or show evidence of success, and devise plans for improving the condition...."

The Committee followed through and held all three meetings in 1977-78. The ultimate goal for each consultation was to aid and/or encourage the participants to fashion and implement "affirmative action plans." One result was the development of an affirmative action plan by the Christian Church Services unit in Missions Building, Indianapolis, Indiana. Other units were reaffirmed in efforts they had made up to that time.

## THE STRUGGLE TO SECURE AND EMPOWER BLACK EXECUTIVES

Since the advent of the National Convocation in 1970, a handful of African-American Disciples of Christ have been employed in Regional and General Church organizations, and provided with a modest degree of upgrading and empowerment.

John R. Compton, a successful pastor from Cincinnati, Ohio, broke precedent in 1968-1970 by moving from a regional staff position in

Cleveland, Ohio, to Directorship of General Reconciliation. He was the first African-American Assistant to the General Minister President as well as Administrative Secretary of the National Convocation.

After returning to his Cincinnati, Ohio, pastorate in 1972, he accepted the call from Indiana to become the first African-American Disciples Regional Minister in 1977. Later, in 1982, following the December 1981 retirement of Kenneth A. Kuntz, head of the Division of Homeland Ministries, Compton became the first African-American to become the President of a program unit. Compton's movement and empowerment within the institutional structures set an unusual precedent.

The Division of Overseas Ministries was the first major program unit to employ a African-American professional as a department executive. The action occurred in 1975 when Anne Douglas, Staff Director for the Interreligious Foundation for Community Organization in New York City, was employed as the Executive Secretary of the Department of Latin America and the Caribbean.

William Hannah of Cleveland, Ohio, followed in 1976 to become DHM's first Black Department Executive Secretary. He succeeded Loyal Northcot as head of the evangelism and membership thrust of the General Church.

But the upward mobility of African-American women has been even more difficult. In 1984 Julia Brown, who had been serving as the director of the General Church's "Mother-to-Mother" program, was upgraded to the Division of Overseas Ministries as a Vice-President—a "first" for an African-American Disciples of Christ woman in charge of personnel.

Finally, on January 1, 1988, Janice Newborn, who had been serving as Director of Program Implementation for the Department of Church Women since 1983, became the first African-American woman to head a DHM department. She succeeded Frances S. Craddock as the Executive for the Department of Church Women.

The Convocation endorsed each of these developments in the increase of African-American professional staff because it enhanced both the work of the General Church and the fulfillment of Convocation objectives.

## CONVOCATION TESTED

The National Convocation Board of Trustees was given a rigorous test in August 1985 during the Des Moines, Iowa, General Assembly when the prospects of employing Cynthia Hale of Brunswick, Georgia, as the Associate General Minister and Administrative Secretary of the National Convocation occurred.

The basic claim made by a group of African-American Disciples leaders was that the General Minister and President had not secured adequate advice and counsel from the National Convocation.

Cries of White racism were on one hand heard while others saw Black Disciples of Christ sexism. The incident left an unsavory taste in everyone's mouth.    Hale's name was eventually withdrawn from nomination. The search to fill the office continued.[1]

The Board of Church Extension enabled healing by releasing its Senior Vice-President, Raymond E. Brown, from a major portion of his responsibilities to also serve as Interim Administrative Secretary of the National Convocation while the search continued for an Administrative Secretary. Brown's administrative skills, past service to the Convocation and integrity enabled a peaceful resolve. John R. Foulkes was called to the position of Administrative Secretary of the National Convocation February 1986.

## CONVOCATION/NATIONAL BENEVOLENT ASSOCIATION JOINT TASK FORCE

One of the most successful collaborative actions between the National Convocation and a major Disciples of Christ program unit—outside of the merger of Conventions and staffs agreements—has concerned stewardship. Crusades for a Christian World Funds were used by a "National Convocation of the Christian Church/National Benevolent Association of the Christian Church Joint Task Force on Black Church Work."

Soon after 1946, there was a campaign to raise money to build "a home for Negro aged and a home for Negro children. An NBA/National Christian Missionary Convention task force was established. However, when the Conventions merged, NBA considered the Convocation the successor to the Convention and thus a joint custodian of the funds. The amounts requested were $100,000 for a Home for Negro Children and $80,000 for a Home for Negro Aged. The amounts actually received were $25,292.68 for the children's home and $31,631.77 for the home for the aged or a total of $56,924.45.

By June 30, 1958, additional gifts and interest earnings increased the totals to $30,717.05 for the children's home and $38,399.85 for the home for the aged, or a total of $69,116.90. By "freezing" the two accounts June 30, 1961 at the point of their original gifts; establishing an income fund; and putting the excess balances of the two Crusade funds in that account, resources in the income account were used to make selected benevolent grants to indigent aged Blacks and children who had been screened by the leadership of two Black Disciples of Christ congregations.

By March 31, 1977, the fund accounts stood as follows:

Negro Income Fund ............ $16,721.80

Negro Children's Fund ....... $25,399.95

Negro Aged Fund ................ $34,402.74

GRAND TOTAL .................... $76,524.49

The task force used these funds to: (a) help establish facilities and experimental services to disadvantaged children and youth; (b) seconded Araminta Smith to be a consultant on the social service needs of all NBA facilities and (c) merged the residual funds so that other full-time African-American staff could be employed.[2] As a result, Norma R. Ellington-Twitty and Patricia Clark were added to the NBA staff. Araminta Smith was a professor at St. Louis (Missouri) University when she was hired in 1978. Smith died in 1988.

The Task Force has continued to function with work on other mutual concerns of NBA and the National Convocation. But more importantly, building on the September 6, 1958, recommendations of the National Christian Missionary Convention's "special committee," the goal of building a special home for African-American aged and children was discarded. The Joint Task Force was revived in 1976 with the National Convocation pressing for an opening up of all services and practices within NBA. A creative use of Crusade funds was to use them to accomplish this ultimate goal.

## CHAPTER EIGHTEEN

# AND THE BEAT GOES ON

"...Martin Luther King was a drum major and as drum majors are prone to do, he stood out in front of the movement and helped set and maintain the cadence.... The drum major has to be a leader. No one stands in front of the drum major. He or she may not be able to play the music but the drum major must know the music which is to be played.

The marchers depend on the drum major to point the way yet the marchers must march and keep the beat. There have been many drum majors who have stood out in the forefront. Some heads were chopped off, others were fed to lions, some fell from dreaded diseases far from places called home... At least one was hanged on a cross...

But somehow the world has not learned that though you get rid of the drum major you don't stop the music. The beat goes on...
—*AND THE BEAT GOES ON, excerpt from address delivered by Raymond E. Brown in Missions Building chapel, Indianapolis, Indiana, Martin Luther King, Jr. Day of Observance, January 15, 1979*

"He that findeth his life shall lose it; and he that loseth his life for my sake shall find it."
—*(Matthew 10:38)*

For many the servant hood role of the National Convocation presents a fascinating challenge. For others the mandate only brings frustration and disillusionment. Yet "the beat goes on." And if there is to be a true partnership in the Christian mission, there will be much more sharing required. And, as Raymond E. Brown points out, some will have their heads chopped off, die from dreaded diseases far from home, or be crucified like the Master.  There is so much more to share about the National Christian Missionary Convention/National Convocation journey which cannot be shared in this treatise.

## THE PARTNERSHIP IN THE MISSION TO MAKE MORE DISCIPLES

Workshops and seminars on evangelism take place during every National Convocation Biennial Session. In addition to these events, there is a story that could be told about participation with Eastern Seaboard Assemblies. During the mid-1960's evangelism institutes were held.  Under the leadership of R.L. Saunders a Convocation team of ministers conducted a two-week evangelistic mission to Jamaica in 1973. "Good News Festivals," the idea of the Convocation board of trustees, were held in 1982-83. These festivals became a reality through the efforts of Convocation representative Oscar Haynes and then DHM general staff member John Foulkes. Ten cities throuhout the United States became the site of thirteen two-to-three day preaching/teaching seminars that were designed by Black Disciples  for the full Churches participation.

The Convocation has rejoiced in the growth of predominantly Black Convocation-related congregations like Light of the World in Indianapolis, Indiana; Park Manor in Chicago, Illinois; United in Detroit, Michigan; Williamsburg in Brooklyn, New York; and Mississippi Boulevard in Memphis, Tennessee. Keith E. Clark observed the life and work of Light of the World (i. e. then Second Christian) under the leadership of its pastor, T. Garrott Benjamin, in 1982 and described it as "Success With an Old Message."[1] The Convocation has encouraged this kind of "success." "And the beat goes on."

## PARTNERSHIP IN THE MISSION TO PRESERVE THE LEGACY OF BLACK DISCIPLES OF CHRIST

One of the first task forces established was the Black Disciples of Christ Historical Materials Committee which met February 5, 1973. Its task was to:

1.  Orient Black Disciples to their Christian heritage in the United States;

2. Enlighten White Disciples as to the contribution made to the movement of Black Disciples;

3. Inform non-Disciples about the involvement of Blacks in the Disciples of Christ church mission; and

4. Motivate the academic research community to do more basic research in the field.

Through the dedicated efforts of Robert L. Jordan, Detroit, Michigan; William Alphin, St. Louis, Missouri; C. C. Mosley, Jackson, Mississippi; Robert H. Peoples, Indianapolis, Indiana; Herbert H. Lambert, and Orville W. Wake of the Christian Board of Publication in St. Louis, Missouri; and Marvin D. Williams of the Disciples of Christ Historical Society in Nashville, Tennessee, the journey toward realizing the four objectives was begun. The CMF/CWF study booklet, THE UNTOLD STORY, was produced in 1975. Soon after came the BLACK DISCIPLES LEGACY SERIES which was intended to be only the first of a series of biographical sketches of many faithful servants in the church.

Finally, in 1979, under the stimulus of Joseph Saunders, then Director of Information in the Office of Communications for the General Office, a Commission on Convocation Publications was established for the expressed purpose of publishing materials under the auspices of the Convocation. Concern for the marketing aspects of publication were raised by the Board of Trustees in 1983-84. But the basic purposes of this Commission are yet to be realized. Under the guidance of Administrative Secretary John R. Foulkes and President Alvin O. Jackson, the concern for Convocation publications was revived. "And the beat goes on."

## MOBILIZING EXISTING RESOURCES

During the Convocation presidential administrations of Ozark Range, Sr. (1978-80) and T. Garrott Benjamin, Jr. (1980-82), a project for the preservation of Black Disciples of Christ legacy was instituted with somewhat low visibility. A task force chaired by Alvin Jackson, Memphis, Tennessee, devised a plan for the establishment of the Preston Taylor National Convocation Endowment Fund. The ultimate goal was a principal of $2,500,000.

Individual gifts from some of the leadership and a donation from earnings from the Greenwood Cemetery operations would be used to put the program in motion in 1980. Earnings from the principal were to placed under the stewardship of the Board of Trustees. On an annual basis, such funds were to be merged with the resources of a selected program unit to carry out a program project. The trustees were to select that program unit and project.

In 1984, through the urging of William Hannah, successor to William K. Fox, Sr., as the Convocation executive staff, the Endowment Fund idea was given new life. Oscar Haynes of Washington, D. C. was hired as a field agent and the Christian Church Foundation and the Division of Homeland Ministries development office gave guidance. The goals of this important venture are unfulfilled. The potential is great. "And the beat goes on."

## PARTNERSHIP IN THE MISSION WITH THIRD WORLD PEOPLES

Through the revival of the concern for Black consciousness in the 1960's, African-American Disciples of Christ gained a new appreciation and understanding of their connection with other peoples throughout the world—especially those in the Third World. This was recognized early in the life of the National Convocation through intentional planning of programs for the Biennial Sessions and the careful selection of ways to dramatize this interest. This connection with other peoples was by a Task Force on Third World Relationships. Cooperation was secured from the Division of Overseas Ministries of the Christian Church (Disciples of Christ).

In June 1972, through the observation of Thomas Griffin, then Director of Promotion for the General Reconciliation Committee, and with the cooperation of DOM staff Joseph Smith and Robert Thomas, newly selected Convocation Administrator, William K. Fox, became a member of the first Disciples of Christ "Church-to-Church Visitation" to the churches in Asia. Later, in July 1975, the National Convocation collaborated with Robert Nelson and the Department of Africa, in sending the Convocation executive on a visitation of church work in Kenya, Zambia, and Tanzania of East Africa; Ghana, Liberia and Dakar of West Africa. Valuable relationships were developed between African churches, the Administrative Secretary and the National Convocation of the Christian Church.

An annual spring visitation to Jamaica for the synod meeting of the Disciples of Christ became an established relationship—usually through the Administrative Secretary, Board of Trustees President, or an appointee. Then, there was cooperation in getting Jamaican representation to the Convocation Biennial Session and/or the General Assembly of the Christian Church (Disciples of Christ). Effort was made to support the Jamaican church in realizing some of its mission objectives.

On May 6-10, 1974, the Convocation collaborated with the Division of Overseas Mission to send Samuel W. Hylton, Jr. of St. Louis, MO to Kyoto, Japan as a Disciples representative to the Consultation on "Minority Issues in Japan and Mission Strategy". Hylton returned to share an informative and inspiring report. He noted:

Koreans in Japan, even after World War II, have lived continuously in an oppressed condition. Their basic rights have not been fully acknowledged in such fields as education, employment, marriage, housing, social security, citizenship, etc...

The denial of humanity and self-respect to large masses of the world is an injustice which can no longer be tolerated...[2]

The strategic placement of Convocation representatives in Third World situations caused them to return and share their broadened perspectives and understanding. Others went to India, Asia and Africa. For a short time, the Convocation joined the Division of Overseas Ministries in sending Thomas Griffin to Kitwe, Zambia for a sabbatical at Mindolo Institute. Later the Convocation considered the support of a vocational education project at the Institute. "And the beat goes on."

## CRITIQUE OF THE "DRUMMER"

The Convocation was hardly five years old before there were indications of a need for in-depth evaluation and study of priorities. It was clear to many that although the Conventions had merged and the Convocation was created (in the minds of some, as an interim arrangement) there were still many needs which had to be dealt with. The Convocation was a new style of churchmanship. Its leadership was biblically based and inclined toward the whisperings of the Holy Spirit. But the path of servant hood was difficult. And the need to function as the drum major—for both African-American and Anglo-American Disciples— was a demanding one.

Some of the "restless ones" called for a "new deal" during the 1976 Biennial Session in Nashville, Tennessee. But many thought their call for something like an all-African-American unit smacked of an "old way" once tried and found wanting. October 19-20, 1976, the

Convocation Board of Trustees launched a Task Force on Convocation Study. Its membership was Irving Allen, Chairman, Hawkins, Texas; Lucile Compton, Cincinnati, Ohio; Delores Carpenter, Washington, DC; Daniel Heath, Rockford, Illinois; Alvin Jackson, Indianapolis, Indiana; Timothy James, Cleveland, Ohio; Clarence Johnson, Jackson, Mississippi; Robert H. Peoples, Indianapolis, Indiana; Oscar Haynes, Washington, DC; and Kenneth Teegarden, Indianapolis, Indiana. The staff researchers were Effie Blair, Raymond Brown, Enoch Henry, Ozark Range, Sr., Joseph Saunders, and the Administrative Secretary, William K. Fox, Sr.

The trustees provided funds for the task force to employ Speed Leas of Bloomfield, Michigan, as the process consultant, and Joseph T. Taylor of Indianapolis, Indiana, his Associate. Both were skilled professionals in assisting non-profit groups like the Convocation to access their life and work.

The Task Force took nearly a year to study the following: (a) Convocation goals; (b) structure and relationship to the church; (c) what the clergy and laity wanted; (d) progress in the implementation of official church commitments; and (e) the participation of the Convocation in the life of the Disciples of Christ. Thirteen recommendations were made.

In general, they called for a strengthening of the Convocation office and staff, coordination of professional staff services to predominantly African-American congregations, and general improvement of communication at all levels. It also concluded that the Convocation was a necessary vehicle for getting most of these things done. The recommendations inferred that initiative would come mainly from the Office of the General Minister and President. It was then shared with regional church staffs, and Convocation-related congregational leadership.

Five years later, in May 1982, under the leadership of Administrative Secretary William Hannah and the Board of Trustees, a suggestion for improvement was drafted called "Proposal for Reorganization for Maximum Effectiveness of Black Disciples as Members of the Christian Church (Disciples of Christ)." The concept gave priority to "Regional and cluster convocations (which) will organize, using the National Convocation's operational procedures."

Suggestions were made for a close alignment with Regions in devising program project and selecting board memberships. It was suggested that funding would be mainly through a variety of individual annual "memberships."

William Hannah, the principal advocate of this arrangement, left the office of administrative secretary and associate general minister and president in 1984 to be the senior pastor at Faith United Christian Church, Indianapolis, Indiana. The idea had been discussed during the 1984 biennial session in Montgomery, Alabama. The proposal was tabled because there was lack of leadership on follow-through. But "the beat goes on."

Woodie W. White, (now a Methodist bishop), but formerly the Executive Secretary of the Commission on Religion and Race for the United Methodist Church, wrote something on "The Future of Black Caucuses" in the Winter/1975 issue of RENEWAL which still may bear thoughtful reading in the late twentieth century. (For, indeed, the National Convocation of the Christian Church (Disciples of Christ) is essentially a "caucus.")

Today, while Black caucuses are still maintained within the predominantly white churches, the emphasis seems to have changed considerably. The aggressive confrontational style reminiscent of the late sixties has all but disappeared. Funds are more difficult to raise, and almost none of the caucuses developed any sizable support from their Black constituencies, since they were largely   supported by denominational sources...

In interviewing various caucus representatives, it is clear they still see the need for the Black caucus. However, it appears the emphasis is shifting from the national scene to the empowerment of the local church, and greater concentration on the local judicatories. It has also become clear to some caucus leaders, that greater efforts must be put on increasing lay participation in the caucus movement. Other caucus leaders are trying to help their denomination address itself to the shortage of Black clergy. One Black caucus is concentrating its focus on economic development.

Oddly enough, few are addressing themselves to the issue of white racism. Even though, one caucus leader says, "things are worst today than they were five years ago."[3]

Though White's observations were made more than a decade ago they have a strange and disturbing contemporary relevance.

## HISPANIC AND ASIAN BROTHERS AND SISTERS

Hispanic and Asian brothers and sisters have benefited much from both the good and bad experiences of the National Christian Missionary Convention/National Convocation. The evolution of the name for the church-wide structure dealing with African-American concerns has been: the Committee on Black Church Work, the Committee on Black and Hispanic Concerns, the Committee on Racial Ethnic Inclusiveness and Empowerment (as of 1988). These name changes reflect the growth in the comprehension of our common humanity.

While functioning as the Associate General Minister and President in the late 1980's, John Foulkes chaired the Committee on Racial Ethnic Inclusiveness and Empowerment. The committee fashioned the substance of a General Church resolution on the theological foundations of "The Inclusive Church" and their practical implications for the individual, the congregation, the Region, and General manifestations of church.[4] How the church deals with questions raised by such deliberations will no doubt shape the direction of the Convocation's future partnership in the Christian mission.

In April 1988, the Hispanic membership of the newly named Committee on Racial Ethnic Inclusiveness and Empowerment, opened the meeting with the following announcement:

> The Hispanic Caucus perceives a structural problem within our church, the Christian Church (Disciples of Christ) in the United States and Canada. We believe our ecclesiastical structure inhibits our full and genuine participation as Hispanics. This realization has led us to a decision to address from our perspective the structure of our church. We will be initiating a process by which we can articulate this structural problem and address it, a process which will require your prayers and support...

The Hispanic members said "We want to address the root causes which do not lie within our Committee and which this Committee cannot address."

American Asian representatives affirmed the purposes of the Committee and they're continuing support and membership. Alvin O. Jackson, President of the National Convocation, stated:

The Board of Trustees of the National Convocation identifies with the hurt expressed by the Hispanic Caucus and acknowledges their right to take a leave from participation on this Committee as individuals who represent the Hispanic constituency. However, the Board of Trustees of the National Convocation wishes to affirm the purpose of C.R.E.I.E. and affirm our on-going participation in the life and work of the Committee.

"And the beat goes on." Through the dynamic interaction of concerned church leaders like African-Americans, His-panics, American Asians and Anglo-Americans a clearer vision of our partnership in the mission will be achieved. "And the beat goes on."

# NOTES

P. 1. Brenda Marie Cardwell, *Three Concerns of Black Disciples of Christ from 1917 To 1969*, Master of Divinity degree thesis, Lexington, Kentucky, 1981.

P. 2. James L. Blair, *The National Convention Facing Integration*, Bachelor of Divinity degree thesis, School of Religion, Butler University, Indianapolis, Indiana, 1958.

1. 1. Ibid., p. 1ff.

1. 2. W. E. Garrison & A. T. Groot, *The Disciples of Christ: A History*, Christian Board of Publication, St. Louis, Missouri, p. 468.

1. 3. Charles Richard Reed, *A Sketch Of The Religious History Of Negroes In The South*, Papers of the American Society of Church History, Second Series, Vol IV., G.F. Putnam's Sons, 1914, New York, New York, p. 181.

1. 4. Ibid, p. 185.

1. 5. B. E. Mayes & J. W. Nicholson, *The Negro's Church*, Institute of Social & Religious Research, 1933 p. 3.

1. 6. G. G. Parsons, *Inside View Of Slavery*, J. P. Jewett & Co., 1855, p. 256.

1. 7. T. D. Weld, *American Slavery As It Is*, Anti-Slavery Society, 1839, New York, New York, p. 24.

1. 8. Parsons, op. cit., p. 24.

1. 9. Zenobia Turner (Daughter of I.Q. Hurdle), Unpublished history of the Texas Christian Missionary Convention (Personal Files), Dallas, Texas.

1.10. Tri-State District Convention, *Program Book, Centennial Celebration Of The Tri-State District Convention, July 21–25, 1982*, Martinsville, Virginia, pp. 34–36.

1.11. Graves, Hancock, Nolan, Russell, *We Are Family*, Family Reunion mimeographed program book, June 30, 1984, p. 7.

2. 1. American Christian Missionary Society *Minutes*, 1867, p. 14.

2. 2. Robert Hayes Peoples, *Historical Development Of Negro Work And Its Relation To Organized Brotherhood Life*, unpublished, undated article.

2. 3. J.B. Lehman, *Letter To Major & Mrs. J. Jarvis On The Establishment Of Jarvis*, Division of Homeland Ministries Files, Disciples of Christ Historical Society, June 29, 1912, Typewritten, Nashville, Tennessee.

2. 4. Albert Berry, *Letter to J. B. Lehman on Proposed Salary For Jarvis Job*, Division of Homeland Ministries Files, Disciples of Christ Historical Society, July 1, 1912, Nashville, Tennessee.

2. 5. J. B. Lehman, *Letter of Response to Albert Berry's Salary Protest*, Division of Homeland Ministries Files, Disciples of Christ Historical Society, July 6, 1912, Typewritten, Nashville, Tennessee.

2. 6. J. B. Lehman, *Letter to Albert Berry with Official Job Offer*, Division of Homeland Ministries Files, Disciples of Christ Historical Society, July 22, 1912, Typewritten, Nashville, Tennessee.

2. 7. Ibid.

2. 8. J. B. Lehman, *Letter to J. N. Ervin of General Counsel*, Division of Homeland Ministries Files, Disciples of Christ Historical Society, March 23, 1914, Typewritten, Nashville, Tennessee.

2. 9. Benjamin Quarles, *The Negro In The Making Of America*, Collier Macmillan Publishers, 1987, Second Revised Edition, New York, London, C. 6.

3. 1. Lerone Bennett, Jr., *Before The Mayflower, A History Of Black America*, Penguin Books, 1984, New York, New York, p. 441 ff.

3. 2. Ibid.

3. 3. A. T. DeGroot, *The Convention Among Disciples Of Christ*, Texas Board of Christian Churches, 1955, Fort Worth, Texas, p. 39.

3. 4. National Christian Missionary Convention *Minutes*, 1917, United Christian Missionary Society File, Disciples of Christ Historical Society, Nashville, Tennessee.

3. 5. Blair, Op. Cit., pp. 35–40.

3. 6. Ibid.

4. 1. National Christian Missionary Convention, *Minutes Of The Third Convention*, 1919, United Christian Missionary Society Files, Disciples of Christ Historical Society, Nashville, Tennessee.

4. 2. National Christian Missionary Convention, *Minutes Of The Fourth Convention*, 1920, United Christian Missionary Society Files, Disciples Of Christ Historical Society, Nashville, Tennessee.

4. 3. Ibid.

4. 4. Ibid

4. 5. *The Gospel Plea*, July 1, 1922, Vol. XXII, No. 563.

4. 6. Ibid.

4. 7. Ibid.

4. 8. J. B. Lehman, *Letter to Episcopal Bishop Theodore D. Bratton*, United Christian Missionary Society Files, Disciples of Christ Historical Society, Nashville, Tennessee.

5. 1. National Christian Missionary Convention Minutes, 1917, Op. Cit.

5. 2. Ibid.

5. 3. National Christian Missionary Convention Minutes, 1920, Op. Cit.

5. 4. P. C. Washington, *The Christian Plea "Jarvis: A Crusading College"*, June 1946, Vol. LV. No. 6., St. Louis, Missouri, pp. 7–8.

5. 5. C. A. Berry, Jr. & E. W. Rand, *An Abstract Of Negro Education In The Disciple Brotherhood, A comparative Study,* 1939, Indiana University Bureau of Educational Research, Bloomington, Indiana, p. 29.

5. 6. Ibid.

6. 1. Joint Executive Committee, *Minutes,* February 12, 1930, National Convention & United Christian Missionary Convention, Indianapolis, Indiana.

6. 2. Ibid.

6. 3. Ibid.

6. 4. Bertha Mason Fuller, *Sarah Lue Bostic: Minister And Missionary,* 1949, Author, Little Rock, Arkansas, pp. 21–22.

6. 5. *The Christian Plea,* April 10, 1939, Vol. XLVI. No. 36., p. 6.

6. 6. Ibid., July 30, 1940, p. 1.

6. 7. Ibid., April 1941.

6. 8. Ibid, March 1943, p. 7.

6. 9. *The Student Voice,* December, 1945, Vol. 4. No. 5., p. 4.

7. 1. Convention of the Colored Churches of Christ *In* South Carolina, *Minutes of the Sixty-Eighth Annual Convention,* October 4–6, 1939, mimeographed.

7. 2. R. H. Peoples, *Report Of The National Secretary Of Negro Churches To The TwentySixth National Christian Missionary Convention,* 1943 Columbus, Ohio.

7. 3. Blair, Op. Cit., p. 81.

8. 1. National Christian Missionary Convention, *Staff Report,* August 19–25, 1957, mimeographed, p. 31.

8. 2. Ibid., p. 26.

8. 3. National Christian Missionary Convention, *Welcome Program Thirty-Eighth Annual Convention,* August 16–22, 1954, St. Louis, Missouri, p. 16.

10. 1. *The Jarvisonian,* September, 1962, Vol. V., No. 4., p. 1.

10. 2. National Christian Missionary Convention, *Minutes Of The Forty-Sixth Annual Assembly,* August 20–26, 1962, Williamsburg Christian Church, Brooklyn, New York.

10. 3. National Christian Missionary Convention, *Report Of The Commission On "This Ministry" To The FortySixth Annual Assembly,* 1962, p. 2.

11. 1. *The Christian Plea,* December 1963, Vol. 52., No. 4., p. 1.

11. 2. National Christian Missionary Convention, *The Forty-Eighth Annual Assembly Program Book,* August, 1964, Rockford, Illinois.

11. 3. William K. Fox, Sr., *An Historical Perspective, Design For Renewal And Growth Of The Christan Church (Disciples Of Christ) Among Negroes,* 1966, National Christian Missionary Convention, p. 5.

12. 1. *The Christian Plea,* December, 1961, Vol. 50., No. 4.

12. 2. "This Ministry" Report, Op. Cit.

13. 1. Christian Church (Disciples of Christ), *Yearbook And Directory,* 1972, Indianapolis, Indiana p. 181.

13. 2. Ibid., p. 182.

13. 3. John R. Compton, *Response To Resolution No. 19 By Congregations,* General Units, Institutions, Regional Organizations Of The Christian Church Disciples Of Christ), July 17–20, 1971, Indianapolis, Indiana.

13. 4. Ibid.

13. 5. Ibid.

14. 1. National Convocation of the Christian Church, *Minutes Of The Second Biennial Assembly,* August 23–27, 1972, Wilson, North Carolina.

14. 2. Christian Church (Disciples of Christ), *World Call, "Black Disciples: A Special Report,* September, 1973, Vol. 55., No. 8.

14. 3. Lorenzo J. Evans, *What Is Meant By The Black Experience,* A paper for the Black Church Education Committee of the Joint Education Development Project, 1972, Mimeographed, pp. 1–11.

14. 4. Joseph S. Saunders, *Update On The Black Church, "Footprints and Shadows",* July/August, 1976, Vol. IV., No. 7/8., p. 9.

14. 5. Ibid., *"Get Into Action",* March/April, 1977, Vol. V., No. 3/4., pp. 1–2.

15. 1. *World Call,* Op. Cit.

16. 1. Raymond E. Brown, *The Disciple, "Black Congregations: Four Years Have Made A Difference",* March 17, 1974, pp. 9–10.

16. 2. Ibid.

16. 3. Raymond E. Brown, *Services To Black Congregations: Evaluating The Progress,* 1987, Board of Church Extension of the Disciples of Christ, Indianapolis, Indiana.

17. 1. *Des Moines Register,* August 6, 1985.

17. 2. Donald O. Legg, *Memorandum To The National Benevolent Association Executive Committee,* June 8, 1977.

18. 1. Keith E. Clark, *The Disciple, "Success With An Old Message",* May 16, 1982, Vol. 9., No. 10., p. 6.

18. 2. National Convocation of the Christian Church, *From Here To...,* *Program Book For The Eighth Biennial Session Of The National Convocation,* August, 1984, Montgomery, Alabama, p. 8.

18. 3. Woodie W. White, *Renewal, "The Future Of Black Caucuses",* 1975, Vol. 11., No. 2., p. 14.

18. 4. Christian Church (Disciples of Christ), *Business Item No. 1089,* Progress Report—The Committee On Racial Ethnic Inclusiveness & Empowerment: Image Of The Inclusive Church.

# APPENDICES

## NATIONAL CONVENTION AND NATIONAL CONVOCATION ASSEMBLY BY YEAR, PLACE, PRESIDENT, ADMINISTRATIVE STAFF EXEC.

| YEAR | PLACE | PRESIDENT | ADM. STAFF |
|------|-------|-----------|------------|
| 1917 | Nashville, TN | Preston Taylor | J. B. Lehman |
| 1918 | Nashville, TN | Preston Taylor | J. B. Lehman |
| 1919 | Nashville, TN | Preston Taylor | J. B. Lehman |
| 1920 | Paducah, KY | Preston Taylor | J. B. Lehman |
| 1921 | Hawkins, TX JARVIS | Preston Taylor | J. B. Lehman |
| 1922 | Indianapolis, IN | Preston Taylor | J. B. Lehman |
| 1923 | Kansas City, MO | Preston Taylor | J. B. Lehman |
| 1924 | Chicago, IL (Armour) | Preston Taylor | J. B. Lehman |
| 1925 | Cincinnati, OH (Fifth) | Preston Taylor | J. B. Lehman |
| 1926 | Louisville, KY | Preston Taylor | J. B. Lehman |
| 1927 | Washington, D. C. | Henry L. Herod | Robert Hopkins |
| 1928 | Chicago, IL (Oakwood) | Henry L. Herod | Robert Hopkins |
| 1929 | Winston Salem, N. C. | Henry L. Herod | Robert Hopkins |
| 1930 | Cleveland, Ohio | Henry L. Herod | Robert Hopkins |
| 1931 | Kansas City, Kansas | Henry L. Herod | Robert Hopkins |
| 1932 | Paducah, Kentucky | Henry L. Herod | Robert Hopkins |
| 1933 | Cincinnati, OH (Fifth) | Henry L. Herod | Willard M. Wickizer |
| 1934 | Hannibal, Missouri | Henry L. Herod | Willard M. Wickizer |
| 1935 | Jackson, Mississippi | Henry L. Herod | Willard M. Wickizer |
| 1936 | Tulsa, Oklahoma | J. N. Ervin | Robert H. Peoples |
| 1937 | Dayton, Ohio | L. H. Crawford | Robert H. Peoples |
| 1938 | Knoxville, Tennessee | L. H. Crawford | Robert H. Peoples |
| 1939 | St. Louis, Missouri | L. H. Crawford | Robert H. Peoples |
| 1940 | Nashville, Tennessee | L. H. Crawford | Robert H. Peoples |
| 1941 | Little Rock, AR | R. W. Watson | Robert H. Peoples |

| YEAR | PLACE | PRESIDENT | ADM. STAFF |
|------|-------|-----------|------------|
| 1942 | Kansas City, MO | R. W. Watson | Robert H. Peoples |
| 1943 | Columbus, Ohio | W. H. Taylor | Robert H. Peoples |
| 1944 | Lexington, Kentucky | W. H. Taylor | Emmett J. Dickson |
| 1945 | Nashville, Tennessee | S. S. Myers | Emmett J. Dickson |
| 1946 | Brooklyn, New York | S. S. Myers | Emmett J. Dickson |
| 1947 | Cincinnati, Ohio | S. S. Myers | Emmett J. Dickson |
| 1948 | Detroit, Michigan | S. S. Myers | Emmett J. Dickson |
| 1949 | Edwards, MS | R. H. Davis | Emmett J. Dickson |
| 1950 | Memphis, Tennessee | R. H. Davis | Emmett J. Dickson |
| 1951 | Indianapolis, IN | Blair T. Hunt | Emmett J. Dickson |
| 1952 | Los Angeles, CA | Blair T. Hunt | Emmett J. Dickson |
| 1953 | Roanoke, Virginia | L. L. Dickerson | Emmett J. Dickson |
| 1954 | St. Louis, Missouri | L. L. Dickerson | Emmett J. Dickson |
| 1955 | Dayton, Ohio | R. H. Peoples | Emmett J. Dickson |
| 1956 | Kansas City, MO | R. H. Peoples | Emmett J. Dickson |
| 1957 | Baltimore, MD | R. L. Jordan | Emmett J. Dickson |
| 1958 | Oklahoma City, OK | R. L. Jordan | Emmett J. Dickson |
| 1959 | Dallas, Texas | John Compton | Emmett J. Dickson |
| 1960 | Columbus, Ohio | John Compton | Emmett J. Dickson |
| 1961 | Roanoke, Virginia | William K. Fox | Emmett J. Dickson |
| 1962 | Brooklyn, NY (Wmsbg) | William K. Fox | Emmett J. Dickson |
| 1963 | Detroit, MI (United) | Charles H. Webb | Emmett J. Dickson |
| 1964 | Rockford, IL (Second) | Charles H. Webb | Emmett J. Dickson |
| 1965 | Brooklyn, NY (Styv.) | Eugene W. James | Emmett J. Dickson |
| 1966 | Chicago, IL (PkMan.) | Eugene W. James | Emmett J. Dickson |
| 1967 | Hawkins, Texas | R. L. Saunders | Emmett J. Dickson |
| 1968 | Hawkins, Texas | R. L. Saunders | Emmett J. Dickson |
| 1969 | Lexington, Kentucky | Raymond E. Brown | Emmett J. Dickson |

## NATIONAL CONVOCATION OF C. C. BIENNIAL ASSEMBLIES

| YEAR | PLACE | PRESIDENT | ADM. STAFF |
|------|-------|-----------|------------|
| 1970 | Columbia, Missouri (Christian College) | Raymond L. Brown | John R. Compton |
| 1972 | Wilson, N. CA. (Atlantic Chrs. Col.) | Raymond L. Brown | William K. Fox, Sr. |
| 1974 | Atlanta, Georgia (Spellman College) | Claude Walker | William K. Fox, Sr. |
| 1976 | Nashville, TN (Fisk University) | Samuel W. Hylton | William K. Fox, Sr. |
| 1978 | Little Rock, AR (Convention Center) | Oscar Haynes (First layman) | William K. Fox, Sr. |
| 1980 | Cincinnati, OH (Neth. Hilton- DnTwn) | Ozark Range, Sr. | William K. Fox, Sr. |
| 1982 | Indianapolis, IN (Atkinson Hotel) | T. G. Benjamin | William K. Fox, Sr. |
| 1984 | Montgomery, AL (Civic Center) | Cynthia Hale (First woman) | William W. Hannah Thomas Griffin Raymond E. Brown |
| 1986 | St. Louis, MO (Clarion Hotel) | Charles Faulkner | John R. Foulkes |
| 1988 | Memphis, Tennessee (Convention Center) | Alvin O. Jackson | John R. Foulkes |

NOTE: The National Convention met mainly in churches; registrants stayed in homes. A congregation was host. The Convocation began with a policy of being hosted by a Disciples of Christ affiliated college. In 1974 it switched to Black oriented colleges. The policy of using convention centers/hotels began in 1976. The regional church is the host. (6/88)

## Appendix 2

**ORGANIZATION AND FUNCTIONAL RELATIONS DEVELOPMENT OF THE
NATIONAL CONVENTION/NATIONAL CONVOCATION, 1900- 1970**

| YEAR | Adm. Respon | Exe. Responsible | Administrator | Field Staff |
|---|---|---|---|---|
| 1900 | C.W.B.M. | Anna Atwater (President) | J. B. Lehman (Superintendent) | Deetsey Blackburn |
| 1917 | National Convention Founded | | Rosa Brown Bracy (Gen. Secy.) | P. H. Moss |
| 1920 | UCMS organized and took over Black Church Work | (Presidents) Robert Hopkins; H. McCormick; Daisy Trout; H. Marx (Wo. Exec) | Bessie Chandler | Wm. Alphin; Prince A. Gray; Vance Smith; A. W. Davis |
| 1935 | | W. Wickizer (DHM Exec) | R. H. Peoples (Natl Secy of Negro Work) | |
| 1944 | NCMC hires own staff: gives direct service to Blacks | Ken Kuntz (DHM Exec) T. J. Liggett (Pres UCMS) | E. J. Dickson (Exec Secy) (Staff; resourced NCMC) | Lorenzo Evans; Ruth Ratten; Carnella Barnes; Charles Webb; C. L. Parks Julia Flowers; Anna Jones; Eunice Miller; Lois Mothershed; Alva S. Brown |
| 1959 | UCMS takes over direct services & absorbs NCMC staff | Executives of Home Mission Departments for Evang.; Xns; Educ.; Women | E. J. Dickson (Coordinated field services & resourced NCMC) | Lorenzo Evans; Anna Jones; Charles Webb; Eunice Miller; Bernice Holmes |
| 1969 | NCMC ceases to have an annual assembly; maintains corporation | A. Dale Fiers (1st GMP) | John R. Compton William K. Fox (Ast GMP & Adm Secy) | All Blacks employed directly by each of the respective program units throughout the church |
| 1970 | Convocation structure developed; lodged in the Office of GMP; 1st Convocation session held. | Kenneth Teegarden (2nd GMP) | John R. Compton GMP secures Convocation an administrator who associates with GMP and chairs the Reconciliation and Ethnic/Racial general committees | |

## Appendix 3

**STAR SUPPORTER SEMINARY GRADUATES 1976-1987 BY YEAR, FIRST**

### GRANT RECEIVED AND 1987 STATUS OF MINISTRY

**1976-77**

1. G. L. Brown, Pastoral, Presby. C C., NYC
2. La Taunya Bynum, General Church, DHM Director
3. Cynthia Hale, Pastoral, Ray of Hope, GA
4. Claudia Highbaugh, Institutional, Campus Min, Yale
5. Timothy James, Pastoral, Fifth CC, Cleveland
6. William Lee, Pastoral, Louden Ave. CC, Roanoke
7. Cozell Wilson, Pastoral/Secular, Kinston/Associate, State Govt.
8. Gregg D. Brown, Secular, In circulation

**1977-78**

9. James Crockett, Institutional, Methodist, Nashville
10. Will Crum, Institutional, Army Chaplain
11. Sanford Davis, Pastoral, Overseas Missions
12. Clifton Brodus, Pastoral, Bapt. Ch, Okla. Cty
13. Kizzie Core, Pastoral, Founder, Goldsboro
14. Titus Haynes, Other, Law School

**1978-1979**

15. Levi Braswell, Institutional, Army Chaplain
16. James Demus, Pastoral, Park Manor, Chicago IL
17. Roland Perry, Pastoral, 1st United, Xenia, OH
18. William Edwards, General Church, DHM Director
19. Debbie Thompson, Regional Church, Asso.Sec, IL-WIS
20. Julia Brogdon, Pastoral, Founder-"Freedom"
21. Cornelius Brown, Pastoral, Stuyvesant Hgts. NYC.

**1979-1980**

22.Willie Facen, Pastoral, Willow St., Hannibal

23.Lloyd Facen, Pastoral, Mt. Sinai, N. Lt. Rock

24.Dale Peele, Secular, State, S. CA.

25.L. W. Stewart, Pastoral, Dently Dr.,Dallas, TX

26.John Summers, Secular, Lawyer-Phoenix

27.Delores. Turner, Pastoral, Central CC, K. C., MO

28.Brenda Cardwell, Pastoral, Pastor/Dev, Capitol Ar

**1980-1981**

29.Freddie Hall, Institutional, Military Chaplain

30. Charles. Black, Pastoral, Holly Hill, S. C.

31.Boyze Edwards, Pastoral, E. 6th St., Okl City

32.Joyce Foulkes, Deceased

33.Charlene. Harris, General Church, DHM Director

34. Paula Kelly, Secular, Social Worker

**1981-1982**

35.Larry Goddard, Institutional, Military Chaplain

36.Eugene Lenston, Secular, In circulation

37.Thomas Murray, Pastoral, Gay-Lea, Nashville

38.Perry Spencer, Secular, U.S. Post Off

39.Jack Sullivan, General Church, DHM Director

**1982-1983**

40.Alvin Scott, Other, Unknown

41.Sherm Barclay, Institutional, Prison Work-IL

42.Ralph Steele, Secular, In circulation

# INDEX

(Note: Generally Task Forces, Committees, Commissions, etc. and listed under their own name rather than their parent organization. For example: National Convocation Task Force on Priorities for 1970 is listed under Task Force on Priorities for 1970s)